DISCLAIMER

All statements of fact, opinion, or analysis expressed are those of the author and do not reflect the official positions or views of the CIA or any other U.S. Government agency. Nothing in the contents should be construed as asserting or implying U.S. Government authentication of information or Agency endorsement of the author's views. This material has been reviewed by the CIA to prevent the disclosure of classified information.

The Central Intelligence Agency has not approved, endorsed or authorized this book or the use of the CIA seal, name or initials.

A Life for A Life

A MEMOIR:
My Career in Espionage Working for
the Central Intelligence Agency

HOWARD PHILLIPS HART

Copyright © 2015 Howard Phillips Hart.

All rights reserved. No part of this book may be reproduced, stored, or transmitted by any means—whether auditory, graphic, mechanical, or electronic—without written permission of both publisher and author, except in the case of brief excerpts used in critical articles and reviews. Unauthorized reproduction of any part of this work is illegal and is punishable by law.

All statements of fact, opinion, or analysis expressed are those of the author and do not reflect the official positions or views of the CIA or any other U.S. Government agency. Nothing in the contents should be construed as asserting or implying U.S. Government authentication of information or Agency endorsement of the author's views. This material has been reviewed by the CIA to prevent the disclosure of classified information.

The Central Intelligence Agency has not approved, endorsed or authorized this book or the use of the CIA seal, name or initials.

ISBN: 978-1-4834-3025-6 (sc)
ISBN: 978-1-4834-3024-9 (e)

Because of the dynamic nature of the Internet, any web addresses or links contained in this book may have changed since publication and may no longer be valid. The views expressed in this work are solely those of the author and do not necessarily reflect the views of the publisher, and the publisher hereby disclaims any responsibility for them.

Any people depicted in stock imagery provided by Thinkstock are models, and such images are being used for illustrative purposes only.
Certain stock imagery © Thinkstock.

Lulu Publishing Services rev. date: 04/24/2015

Acknowledgement

This book would not exist were it not for the constant encouragement, support, and hard work of my wife, Jean Hardy Hart, to whom I owe endless thanks.

DEDICATION

For Susan, Colin, and Guy – who served with me – my deepest thanks.

Contents

1. Prologue 1
2. India and Return to the Philippines 23
3. Entering CIA 35
4. Back to South Asia 47
5. The Persian Gulf 63
6. Iran 69
7. Iran's Maneuvering through a Revolution 79
8. The Iran Rescue Mission 91
9. Islamabad, Pakistan: The Afghan War 107
10. The Counter Narcotics Center 125
11. Postscript 135

1

PROLOGUE

The paratrooper jogged down the dusty pathway leading from the internment camp to the beach. Tucked under his left arm was a young boy of about five who had just been rescued from a Japanese prison camp. Under his right arm he carried a Tommy gun. As he ran along, the paratrooper – who had just seen thousands of starving American prisoners – kept saying "I'll get you home kid, I'll get you home." Arriving at the amphibious tractor that would carry the boy and over 2000 other American and Allied prisoners to safety behind American lines, the paratrooper handed the boy up into the willing arms of US Army soldiers who crewed the Amtrak. The trooper then turned around and ran back into the internment camp, his name unknown to the little boy or to his parents.

That soldier would never know that the words "I'll get you home kid" would lead the boy - when he grew up - to join the National Clandestine Service of the CIA, America's espionage service. By the time the boy was in his late teens he knew that he had been given his life by his country - and believed that he owed his country a life in return.

MANILA - BEFORE WORLD WAR II

For expatriate Americans, life in the Philippines before World War II was in many ways an idyllic existence. Americans sent to the Philippines by their companies enjoyed a lifestyle that few people in the United States could emulate. Large colonial style bungalows were the norm, as was a staff of household servants responsive to one's every need. Life revolved around the various clubs – which ranged from the Manila Polo Club, the Army and Navy Club, the Manila Yacht Club – and an endless round of cocktail and dinner parties in private residences. With America still recovering from the Great Depression, the opportunity to live a quasi-sybaritic lifestyle made putting up with the tropical heat easy.

Manila had a large colony of American businessmen, American military officers and American civilians working for the US-dominated Philippine Government. From the mid-1930's onward it was the stated purpose of the United States Government to grant the Philippines full independence by 1946. In fact the United States had grafted the entire American system of government on the Philippines, which by World War II had an elected president, an elected Congress and the full range of government agencies. A country-wide system of public education had been introduced soon after the United States took over the Philippines from Spain. The Philippines was not a colony in the way that the British, Dutch and French governments treated their overseas possessions. It was true that American administrators in the Philippines exercised ultimate control over the country, but they did so fully cognizant of the fact that the whole reason for their presence was to prepare the Philippines for independence.

There had been considerable criticism in the United States in the very early 20th Century of President McKinley's decision to take and keep the Philippines as a possession once it had been wrested from Spain as a consequence of the Spanish-American war. Such criticism was exacerbated by the fact that once the Philippines had been taken from Spain, which had ruled the islands for over 300 years, the U.S. had to suppress what was called the "Philippine Insurrection" fought by Filipinos who believed they had the right to establish their own independent country once Spain had departed. The "Insurrection" evolved into a nasty anti-guerrilla war which required United States to take to the field for several years to defeat the poorly armed and led Philippine insurgents. Remarkably, once the Insurrection was over and it was clear to the educated class of Filipinos that the United States intended to withdraw from the Philippines after a brief period of "nation building," relations between Filipinos and Americans were very good.

The United States maintained a relatively small military presence in the Islands. A major responsibility of much of that presence was to create a Philippine Army, able, it was hoped, to defend the Philippines once Independence arrived. Manuel Quezon, the President of the Philippines, hired General Douglas Macarthur – who had retired from American military service – to manage the creation of this new Philippine Army. The very limited number of American troops in the islands was there not to hold down the Filipino people but to bolster the nascent Philippine Army in what was regarded as the very limited likelihood of invasion by a foreign power – principally by Japan.

From the mid-1930s onward war clouds rapidly gathered in the Far East. Japan's invasion of Manchuria, and its later move into China proper, seemed to indicate that the self-styled Japanese Empire could very well plan to invade South East Asia: which meant the Dutch East Indies (now Indonesia); French Indo China, and the British possessions of Malaya and Singapore. The idea that Japan would invade the Philippines, the only significant American presence in the area, seemed to most people to be absurd. The thinking was that however arrogant Japan's military-dominated government might be, the Japanese would never be "foolish" enough to attack the American-held Philippines.

Relations between Japan and the U.S. deteriorated in the late 1930's, and worsened in 1940 and 1941. With hindsight is difficult to believe that the American government, certainly until early 1941, steadfastly refused to acknowledge the possibility of a Japanese invasion of the Philippines. In fact, until several weeks before Pearl Harbor, the American High Commission in Manila – the center of power in the Philippines – was busily reassuring American civilians in the country that there was no possibility of war with Japan. Certainly there was no possibility that the Philippines would be invaded by the Japanese. While the U.S. military quietly withdrew all military dependents from the Islands in early 1941, and the U.S. added a very small number of reinforcements to its Philippine garrison, the American civilian community continued to believe that war with Japan and a Japanese invasion of the Philippines was "impossible."

My father admitted to me many years later that there was a large degree of wishful thinking in turning a blind eye to the possibility of war. No one wanted their life in the pre-war Philippines to come to an end: which it would if American civilians returned to the U.S. in anticipation of war. Life was just too good to believe that there was a very real possibility that war would come to the Philippines. He was also very bitter in criticizing the American High Commission for its repeated assertions that war would not come.

There were probably less than 10,000 American civilians in the Philippines when Pearl Harbor was bombed. Many of these civilians were dependents of businessmen, engineers, bankers – in fact the American population of the Islands represented the entire spectrum of society - bank presidents to prostitutes.

War came to the Philippines within hours of the attack on Pearl Harbor. The American military had long planned, in the event of invasion, to withdraw the bulk of U.S. forces (which included twice as many members of the new Philippine Army as American troops) to the Bataan peninsula, which is one arm of the land encircling the huge Manila Bay, and to the heavily fortified Corregidor Island, which lies like a cork in a bottle at the entrance to the Bay. The plan was that our forces would hole up on the peninsula and on the island until relieving forces arrived from the United States. This War Plan was given the code name "ORANGE," and it assumed, of course, that both the Bataan peninsula and Corregidor Island would have sufficient stocks of food, medicine and ammunition to withstand a protracted siege. They did not. Nor were there sufficient forces available in the United States to rush as reinforcements to the Philippines - quite aside from the fact that the United States Navy was in no position to move troops in large numbers to the Philippines following the disaster at Pearl Harbor.

The American defeat in the Philippines in early 1942 was the largest single surrender of U.S. forces in our history. The defense of Bataan and Corregidor was a heroic one, where undernourished, under-equipped and largely untrained soldiers fought on far longer than the Japanese high command, which was well aware of War Plan ORANGE, had anticipated that they would or could.

With the fall of Bataan and Corregidor all American forces in the Philippines were ordered to surrender. Most did, and spent the remainder of WWII in Japanese prisoner of war camps in the Philippines and Japan. The infamous Bataan Death March was only a preamble to the incredibly harsh treatment our prisoners of war received at the hands of the Japanese Imperial Army. It is not a coincidence that the death rate of American military prisoners in the hands of the Japanese was 7 times higher than was the case with American military prisoners in Germany.

A number of American military personnel, most of whom were not on either Bataan or Corregidor, chose to quite literally "take to the hills and jungles" in the hope of establishing guerrilla units to carry on the war against the Japanese. Without supplies, weapons or money many of these early guerrillas were killed or captured by the Japanese. The handful that survived were subsequently armed by supplies coming in via submarine from Australia, and raised guerrilla organizations that were a serious thorn in the side of the Japanese occupation forces.

Such units, usually composed of Filipinos with a handful of American officers, were to play an unexpected role in my life in CIA.

CIVILIANS INTERNED

The city of Manila, where most American civilians were located, fell to the Japanese without any resistance from United States forces. By January 1942 the Japanese began to round up all Allied civilians to place them in internment camps until the "end of the war."

U.S. military personnel captured by the Japanese were Prisoners of War, and were held in Prisoner of War Camps. Civilians taken into custody by the Imperial Japanese Army were called "internees," and were placed in "Internment Camps." It is a fact that civilian prisoners of the Japanese were far better treated – a relative term - than were American prisoners of war. The major difference is that military POWs were subject not only to starvation but to arbitrary physical brutality, torture and execution. Medical care was non-existent. Speaking generally, civilian prisoners were not subject to torture and beatings except when they broke the regulations imposed by the Japanese. As was the case with military POWs, any civilian internee who was captured after attempting to escape was executed. By and large once the Japanese had rounded up all Allied civilians and placed them in internment camps, the Japanese authorities adopted a policy of general neglect. Food was never adequate, and towards the end of the war the amount of food provided was insufficient to maintain life.

The American Red Cross arranged to have significant amounts of food sent to the Philippines for both POWs and civilian internees. With only one or two exceptions all Red Cross food supplies were confiscated and consumed by the Japanese. This is an interesting point: had the Japanese chosen to allow American Red Cross food supplies to reach their intended recipients the Japanese would essentially not have had to provide food supplies at all. Instead the Japanese chose to confiscate and use all such supplies while providing both POW and internment camps with increasingly inadequate amounts of food, either purchased or confiscated from the Filipino population.

The Imperial Japanese Army violated all the provisions of the Geneva Convention regarding the treatment of POWs. The Japanese were slightly more humane when it came to civilian internees: for example, late in the war the Japanese allowed the names of the Allied internees to be released to Red Cross authorities, and on one occasion allowed the internees to write heavily censored letters to relatives in the U.S. They provided no such information on POWs.

Initially all Allied civilians were herded into an internment camp that the Japanese chose to locate at the University of Santo Tomas, which was in the center of Manila. This meant that thousands of civilians of every age were crowded into a facility that was simply far too small for the number of people involved. The overcrowding at Santo Tomas eventually led the Japanese to establish another camp at a new location south of Manila on the grounds of the University of the Philippines' Agricultural College, which Americans had founded well before the war. This Camp was named for the small fishing village of Los Banos, and was the camp that my parents and I were transferred to early in 1944.

Los Banos

Los Baños is located on the southern shore of the large lake called Laguna De Bay. It is roughly 50 miles south of Manila, and is very much a rural area.

The Camp at Los Baños held about 2,200 Allied prisoners. It was made up of a large number of barracks made of local materials, and was entirely surrounded by barbed wire and Japanese watchtowers from which Japanese soldiers armed with machine guns looked down on the internees. Every morning the entire internee population had to assemble on a large field in the middle of the Camp for roll call, which involved the requirement to bow to the Japanese Commandant and to shout "Banzai" in honor of the Emperor of Japan. Any internee who attempted to escape from the Camp was either killed at the time of his escape attempt or, if the escapee was successful in getting out of the camp, he was generally recaptured and promptly executed publicly, in front of the entire internee population. The normal form of execution was beheading: the internee knelt on the ground while a Japanese soldier – usually the infamous Sergeant Major Konishi, chopped the man's head off with his samurai sword.

Roughly 200 Japanese soldiers provided the guard force. There was a Camp Commandant, an ineffectual Japanese Major who had clearly been picked for the job because he was incapable of serving in a Japanese combat unit. His deputy was a senior Noncommissioned Officer named Konishi who was the de facto head of the Japanese administration. Konishi was a malevolent and murderous individual who went out of his way to abuse and denigrate the internees.

As a practical matter, the Camp was run on a daily basis by a Committee of internees composed of senior American businessmen. The Committee was responsible for organizing the Camp and reported to the Commandant and Konishi. All internees had a job of one kind or another. My father, a banker, wound up as a cook whose daily job was to prepare the thin rice gruel which constituted the bulk of the food provided by the Japanese. My mother's job was to handpick bits of rock, straw and glass from the inferior grade of rice that the Japanese provided. (She sensibly did not remove the insects found in the rice, as they provided a tiny – but valuable – bit of protein.) In addition to poor quality rice the Japanese provided an erratic supply of native vegetables and, very occasionally, meat, coconut oil for cooking, coconuts and fruit. There was no milk or poultry. The internees attempted to grow additional vegetables to supplement the Japanese-issued rations, but these "truck gardens" did not significantly ameliorate the food shortage.

Membership in the Camp Committee, made up of senior businessmen, was a thankless job. Not only did the Committee have the task of dealing with the Japanese authorities, which was distinctly a one-way proposition, but Committee members also had to deal with the inevitable bitches and complaints coming from sections of the internee population. The primary subject, of course, was always the amount and kind of food that was being provided – or rather was <u>not</u> being provided – by the Japanese. There seems to have been a small number of permanent complainers among the internees who consistently demanded that the Committee in some unknown way <u>force</u> the Japanese to improve the quality and quantity of food supplied, and at the same time perpetually complained of favoritism and inequality in the distribution of such food as was available from the camp kitchen. I have pages of closely typed memoranda, saved by my father, attempting to explain to the internees all the steps that the Committee took to try to persuade the Japanese to improve the food situation, and to rebut allegations that some people received more food than others. Apparently there were relatively few such "complainers", but they inevitably fueled growing morale problems amongst the internees.

There was, of course, little privacy in the Camp, which was still too small to house the large number of people being detained. By the time we were liberated there were 2,146 internees in the Camp, living in twenty-six barracks with adjoining very primitive toilet and washroom facilities. The Japanese garrison occupied the few permanent buildings which constituted the Agricultural College.

Time passed slowly at Los Banos, where increasingly the one subject that preoccupied all the internees was the matter of insufficient food. As the war progressed and American forces drew closer and closer to the Philippines, food supplies became less and less adequate. This situation came to a head in late 1944, by which time internees were being issued less than 800 calories a day of food – against a requirement for 1,800 to 2,000 calories per day. All internees were dramatically losing weight, and all became increasingly subject to the diseases that attack people living on a starvation diet. While there were adequate numbers of American doctors and nurses in the camp – they too had been rounded up by the Japanese – there was virtually no medicine of any kind, as Red Cross shipments of medications were all confiscated by the Japanese. As the Camp Committee repeatedly brought to the Commandant's attention, the camp population was slowly dying. Which apparently suited the Japanese.

The Internee Committee was not alone in appealing to the Japanese Commandant and to Konishi, the real power in the camp. For example, the Roman Catholic Bishop of Los Banos, who was responsible for over 800 priests, nuns and other Catholics inside the Los Banos camp, in late 1944, wrote a carefully worded letter to the Commandant citing the problems that were being occasioned by the lack of food supplies. The key phrase in the letter was: "Men and women are wasting away, and all the diseases which spring from food deficiency are becoming, daily, more prevalent."

The Bishop went on to make an interesting point: at the beginning of the war, the Japanese had taken all Allied civilian personnel into what the Japanese defined as "Protective Custody." By doing this – and thus depriving the civilians of the means to take care of their own food and medical requirements – the Bishop noted that the Japanese were assuming the responsibility for providing adequate supplies of food and medicines.

The Bishop went on to say that the Japanese should take immediate action to remedy the desperate problem of starvation, and that they were, in fact, <u>obliged</u> to do so. He also noted that many of the internees, including women, children, and the elderly, were already so debilitated as a result of protracted malnutrition that they would either be permanently disabled or die.

The letter was, of course, ignored, and food supplies continued to be reduced.

Since I was a child of four years of age in 1944, my memories of the Camp are limited to a series of brief vignettes. One of the most vivid is my mother's attempt to provide a Christmas dinner in December of 1944. Somehow she had obtained a 6 inch length of a banana plant: not the bananas, but the stalk of the plant, which was roughly four inches in diameter. She carefully cut the stalk into thin, pancake-shaped pieces which she fried in a bit of coconut oil. I remember her attempting to get me to eat this thoroughly indigestible chunk of vegetation, which I did, and which made both of us violently ill. Not a great Christmas Dinner. Kids my age were on the whole reasonably healthy because in addition to our own rations our parents always gave us a portion of their meager issue of food.

There was a fair amount of "black market" activity in the Camp: people who by some means managed to acquire food sold it at huge profit. Since no one had any real money, "bank checks" were written on scraps of paper – payable after the war. My father told the story of writing a "check" on the back of an old envelope for $200 in payment for one can of Spam: in today's terms that would be over $2,000. Such checks were always presented for payment after we were liberated. And they were almost always honored in the United States after the war.

There is no question that by January 1945 the population of the Camp was well on its way to dying of starvation. There was no living thing that internees did not try to eat: rats and mice were delicacy. Any stray dog that happened to wander into the Camp under the barbed wire was promptly captured, killed and eaten. Like all internees I remember the pain of constant hunger. Since I knew nothing but the privations of the internment Camp, hunger seemed to me a fact of life: I assumed that everyone everywhere was always hungry.

There was a fairly large population of children in the Camp, and I remember playing with kids my age and a few years older. The Japanese had decided to round up all Allied religious types in the Islands and placed them in Los Banos, which resulted in adding about eight hundred Catholic priests and nuns to the camp's population. There were so many of "the religious" that they were housed in one particular area of the camp which promptly became known as "Vatican City." This large assembly of religious personnel resulted in the appointment of one of their number as the "Roman Catholic Bishop of Los Banos Internment Camp."

I particularly remember an order of nuns (I believe they were English-speaking Dutch) who wore wonderful white habits which included "flying nun" hats. The nuns took particular charge of children my age, and ran everything from kindergarten classes to simple games: I remember playing "stick ball" (a Camp version of baseball, since we had neither real bats or balls) which featured nuns, in their lovely flowing habits and incredible wide headgear, running from base to base. I always admired these magnificent women, who were endlessly cheerful and totally committed to caring for not just the youngsters but for everyone else in the Camp. How they managed - in the absence of anything approaching real soap and adequate water supplies - to keep their flowing white garments clean and pressed is beyond me.

We kids had all the usual childhood diseases like chicken pox and measles. Our doctors worked heroically to find substitutes for medications – usually a fruitless exercise, but it at least made us think we felt better. Because of our totally inadequate diets all sorts of maladies emerged: Beri Beri and rickets were common. I recall frequent outbreaks of large boils on my body – the result, our doctors said, of the lack of basic vitamins. One of my vignettes is having boils on my neck and rear end punctured and drained without, of course, any anesthesia. It was a messy, bloody and painful affair, and of course the doctor had no suture material so the wounds remained open for some time. Bandages were scraps of clothing torn into strips, boiled, dried, and rolled up.

Another thing I remember is fear of our Japanese guards. While the guards only rarely intentionally abused any internees (except when they were caught trying to escape, or committed some more minor infraction of "the rules") the guard force, which was largely comprised of the very lowest level of Japanese army draftees, demanded and received frequent demonstrations of respect from all internees. This meant that when confronted by a guard one had to bow repeatedly and then raise one's arms in the air and shout "Banzai ... Banzai... Banzai." This was an endless source of amusement for the guards, who knew perfectly well that there was absolute lack of sincerity on the internee's part in saluting the Emperor of Japan. As a practical matter we kids had very little interaction with guards as our parents made sure that we were playing or going to school as far away as possible from the Japanese Commandant's Headquarters and the Japanese guards.

I recall sitting on the ground playing with a simple toy someone had given me. For some reason I had evaded my mother and had chosen to sit down and play near a Japanese machinegun nest located just inside the barbed wire. After a while I noticed that the Japanese had pointed the machinegun at me.

I also saw that they were laughing: apparently the chance to tease a child with the threat of machine-gunning him was tremendously funny. I just stared back. My mother soon found me and, horrified, picked me up, carried me to "safety," and gave my rear end a serious licking. I avoided machinegun nests ever after.

The guards on occasion conducted searches of our quarters looking not so much for forbidden items like radios as they were for personal valuables - which they instantly confiscated. My father told me of hiding his wedding ring in his rectum during a particularly savage shakedown of prisoners. Wristwatches and fountain pens were confiscated by the guards for their own use as soon as internees were taken into camps. Everyone had secret hiding places for the very few personal keepsakes and valuables that they were able to hide from the Japanese.

As a way of passing time many adult internees took courses – given by internees – in everything from the Chinese language to world history. My banker father saved one example of the very comprehensive course materials from a "class" in International Banking that he either took or taught at Los Banos. Children in the Camp ranged from the new-born to kids in their teens.

Amazingly, a number of births occurred in the Camp – of children conceived "inside the wire." Much to the occasional disgust of the "older kids," they had to attend school – taught by the same teachers they had while they were attending classes pre-war. As far as I know no school age children "lost" years of schooling while in the Camp, and High School diplomas were earned and awarded just as though there was no war on. While there were no textbooks or school materials, in general teachers rose to the occasion and modified their courses to operate without them.

Smokers had a particularly difficult time since of course there were no real cigarettes in Camp. My father, always a heavy smoker, told me later that he collected every species of weed (which grew plentifully in the wet tropical environment) and smoked the dried leaves – rolling the "cigarettes" in thin paper from a pocket edition of the King James Bible. When we were finally liberated my Dad weighed 89 pounds, down from his pre-war 185. We were all very skinny, and it was common to see men with their ribs showing plainly through their skin.

LIBERATION

When American forces landed in the Philippines in late 1944 there were roughly 250,000 Imperial Japanese Army troops in the Islands. As it turned out the Philippine campaigns lasted for many months, and in fact had not been concluded by the time of the official Japanese surrender following the dropping of the atomic bombs on Japan. As a practical matter every Japanese soldier had to be killed – there were no mass surrenders even though it was clear that the Americans, with their overwhelming military, air and naval superiority, would eventually prevail.

Prisoners in both Los Banos and Santo Tomas were not allowed to have radio receivers, and thus remained largely ignorant of developments in the war. Fortunately internees contrived to make simple radio receivers in both camps –which, if the Japanese had discovered them, would have resulted in the immediate execution of whoever had possession of the radios. In order to keep the existence of the radios secret, news that was received over the radios was <u>not</u> disseminated to the mass of internees. This meant, of course, that internee's were largely ignorant of developments in the Pacific war, particularly of the inexorable progress of American forces towards the Philippines and Japan. This lack of war news, when coupled with the increasingly difficult conditions imposed on the internees by their Japanese captors, could have had serious adverse consequences on internee morale. According to my parents and autobiographies written by internees after the war, this did not happen. Confidence in an eventual American victory never wavered – although towards the end of three and a half years of imprisonment the question became whether internees would live long enough to witness that victory.

In the last months of 1944 and into very early 1945 the shocking regime of living on 800 or fewer calories a day resulted in the internee population becoming lethargic and demoralized. It is very hard to be optimistic when your body is disintegrating for want of food.

Even before the Americans invaded the Philippine Islands, however, the near presence of our forces became patently obvious because American aircraft began flying over the Camp. Once the U.S. Army landed on the island of Luzon, some distance north of the city of Manila, overflights by American military aircraft became common. I remember my first sight of an American fighter plane over Los Banos: initially I had no idea that the aircraft I saw was American since I had never seen even a photograph of an American military airplane. But then, the other internees did not know them either, as a whole new generation of military aircraft was now operating in the skies over the Philippines – largely unopposed by the Japanese Air Force.

American Headquarters was clearly aware that Los Banos was a Japanese prison camp, since soon after the U.S. invasion of the Islands a pilot flew low over the Camp several times. On his last fly-over the pilot, indifferent to gunfire from the Japanese guard force, performed a slow barrel roll, and dropped his goggles into the Camp. Enclosed in the goggles was a hastily scrawled note with the words "ROLL OUT THE BARREL." Word of this event instantly circulated throughout the Camp, and was taken by a delirious internee population to mean that rescue was close at hand.

Our Japanese guards at first were frantic in their efforts not to let internees see the American aircraft, but they soon abandoned efforts to try to herd all internees into their barracks every time one or more planes flew over the Camp.

Some weeks after the first aircraft made their appearance we began to be able to hear the distant thunder of heavy artillery fire. We later found out this sound was a result of the very difficult month-long battle for the city of Manila – which emerged from the war the most heavily damaged city but for Warsaw.

While there was considerable euphoria over both the sight of the aircraft and the distant sounds of battle, there was also a growing concern on the part of the internee Committee - and in fact all internees - that our Japanese guards were likely to execute all of the prisoners in the Camp before withdrawing and joining a Japanese infantry division that we knew was located a few miles to the south. This concern only grew when food supplies went from grossly inadequate to virtually nothing. While realizing that American forces might soon move south of Manila and capture the territory in which Los Baños lay, there was something close to panic at the thought that a mass execution might take place before we could be liberated.

Years after the war my father told me that he was sure that the Japanese planned to murder the entire population of the camp, disposing of the bodies in a long trench that internees had been ordered to begin digging. I have never been able to prove that this was in fact the intention of the Japanese garrison or of its Headquarters elements. It was certainly what a great many internees believed would happen, and we had seen enough executions of internees by the Japanese to know that our captors were perfectly capable of such an act. Given his later massacre of innocent villagers in Los Banos, Sergeant Major Konishi, the effective commander of the camp's Japanese garrison, could easily have ordered just such an atrocity.

As a result of these fears a very brave American prisoner managed to escape from the Camp and contact a local guerrilla unit. The guerrillas arranged to move him about 40 miles north to the American front lines. He was able to contact American soldiers and was immediately debriefed on the situation in the Camp. Unknown to us at the time, General MacArthur's Headquarters had learned that the Japanese had murdered hundreds of American POWs who were located in a Japanese camp on Formosa. The feeling at MacArthur's Headquarters was that it was at least "very possible" that the Japanese would commit the same atrocity at Los Banos. As a result, a detachment of paratroopers from the 11th Airborne Division was withdrawn from fighting in and near Manila and given the task of liberating the Los Banos Camp - some 40 miles deep in Japanese-held territory.

The rescue mission which followed was a stunning success: a relative handful of American soldiers parachuted into the Camp while Filipino guerrillas attacked it from outside the barbed wire. Virtually the entire Japanese garrison was killed, and all civilian internees were evacuated, in spite of Japanese artillery fire, to the shore of Lake Laguna De Bay where they were picked up by 54 U.S. Army amphibious tractors and removed across the lake to safety.

THE RAID ON LOS BANOS

This successful raid on the Los Banos Internment Camp is studied today at major military academies as an example of how to conduct such an operation. The raid was a triumph of quick and careful planning; the efficient use of resources; the value and use of good intelligence; the importance of Filipino guerilla assistance, the skill of the American soldiers involved; and just plain luck. It was conducted by elements of the 11th Airborne Division, which, until the order was given to conduct the raid, was heavily involved in the fighting for the city of Manila.

The raid involved a covert reconnaissance of the Los Banos camp by a team from the 511th Parachute Infantry Regiment; and subsequent simultaneous attacks on the camp by an American-led Filipino guerilla unit, a company of paratroopers who jumped over the camp, diversionary attacks some distance from the camp by other elements of the 11th Airborne division, and the successful evacuation to safety of all the internees and the attack force The entire operation was planned and executed in less than 48 hours.

The attack began at exactly 7:00 AM, a time selected because it was known that much of the Japanese garrison was involved in their daily calisthenics routine - with their guns secured in the garrison's weapons locker. Information on the Japanese guard force and the location of all Japanese gun positions in the camp was provided to the 11th Airborne Division by an internee who had escaped several days before, and by analysis of reconnaissance photography taken by U.S. planes flying over the camp. The internee reported the desperate food situation being faced by the internees, and the possibility that the Japanese garrison intended to murder the entire internee population. His report was immediately forwarded to General MacArthur's Headquarters, and MacArthur gave the order that the Camp was to be attacked and the internee's liberated as soon as possible.

A small element of the 511th Airborne Infantry Regiment of the 11th Airborne Division crossed Laguna de Bay in native fishing boats on the night of 22/23 February 1944, and linked up with a guerilla unit which was operating very close to the camp. At precisely 07:00 this guerilla unit, reinforced by the men from the 511th, began their attack on Japanese gun positions in the Camp. At exactly the same time about 100 paratroopers from the 511th jumped into a landing zone immediately adjacent to the Camp. The Filipino guerrillas were largely responsible for killing most of the Japanese garrison before the paratroopers even arrived inside the Camp. Once the killing was done, the guerrillas quickly faded back into the surrounding jungle. While the attack was taking place at Los Banos, other elements of the 11th Airborne division began a minor offensive against the Japanese front lines some miles from the Camp: a diversionary attack intended to lead the Japanese to think that a major assault was being executed in that area, and that the Los Banos raid was itself a feint.

With the Japanese garrison disposed of, the plan called for the urgent removal of all of the internees from the camp back to American lines. This was to be accomplished by having a fleet of 54 troop-carrying Amphibious Tractors (Amtracks) trundle into Laguna De Bay in the dark of night, arriving at a beach in the immediate vicinity of the internment camp. Their arrival was timed to coincide with the capture of the camp. In a brilliant feat of night-time dead reckoning navigation over water using only a hand compass, the Amtrak force arrived exactly on time and at exactly the right beach. The Amtracks then proceeded up a dirt road and entered the camp itself.

My memory of the raid – which one way or the other certainly saved our lives – is fairly acute. The entire camp was awaked by the sound of gunfire as the guerrillas fired on and killed the Japanese guards in their watchtowers and machine gun positions on the ground. At the same time there was the noise of a group of C-47 transports which flew over the camp, dropping the paratroopers. The noise level was frightening, and I remember my mother crawling with me to the floor under the rough bed in our barracks building. A few minutes passed and the next thing I recall was the sight of a pair of paratrooper boots standing in the entrance to the barracks and a very loud American voice saying "get the hell out of this building and go to the Amtracks."

I had never seen an American paratrooper. In fact I had never seen an American soldier. While my mother extricated us from under the bed I recall seeing the largest man I had ever seen in my life, armed to the teeth, and clearly not a Japanese guard. The paratrooper repeated his command to leave the barracks building and disappeared. My mother frantically collected our few personal belongings, and we left the barracks building and headed towards the noise of the Amtracks, which were just then entering the camp.

It took only a few minutes to kill the Japanese garrison – although a handful of Japanese soldiers escaped from the camp. Once the gunfire stopped the entire internee population started to gather around the huge Amtracks - which the paratroopers were attempting to fill with people as rapidly as possible. The paratroopers knew that the Japanese 10th Infantry Division was located in the hills just a couple of miles south of the camp, and the possibility of a Japanese counterattack on the small force that had liberated us was a very real one. For that reason the paratroopers had been ordered to get internees into the Amtracks and back down to the beach and across Laguna de Bay and behind American lines as rapidly as possible.

The problem was that the internee's, wildly happy at this 11th hour rescue, were not cooperative. Such was the euphoria that the internee's were hugging soldiers and each other, and were not disposed to immediately climb into the Amtracks. The paratroopers difficulty in rapidly loading us into the vehicles that would take us to freedom was complicated by the fact that some internees refused to leave their barracks – a result of what we now call the "Stockholm syndrome": the fear of leaving familiar surroundings for the unknown. Faced by the refusal of a large number of frightened and stunned internee's to leave their barracks, the order was given to burn the barracks down, and paratroopers were running from building to building with their Zippo lighters. This proved to be an effective means of getting reluctant internees out of the buildings to where the Amtracks were being loaded. Another delay was caused by the internee's determination to collect and pack all of their meager possessions. This amounted to very little, but since it was all each individual had it was considered treasure. This took an inordinate amount of time, and far from being able to quickly load the internee's into the Amtracks, retreat to the lake, and begin the crossing to the American side, the soldiers found that it took nearly 5 hours to gather all of the internees and start them moving to safety.

There was also a delay caused by the fact that the Amtracks could not transport all of the internee's and all of the soldiers involved in one trip: the first Amtracks to leave the camp chugged across Laguna De Bay, dropped off their passengers, and returned for a second trip. All of this took precious time, and we were tremendously fortunate that the Japanese did not launch a counterattack on the camp.

During the business of loading I somehow became separated from my mother, and was swept into the arms of a paratrooper who, impatient with the delay in getting everyone loaded into the machines, decided to carry me bodily down to the lakeshore - where he handed me up into an Amtrack that was just leaving the beach for the American side. It was this paratrooper who kept chanting "I'm going to get you home kid, I'm going to get you home" as he jogged along. The memory of that ride in his arms has been with me ever since, and had an incalculable effect on my life.

Oddly enough my memory of time in the Amtrack as we churned across the Bay was of being very sick. This was caused by the fact that soldiers in the Amtracks were passing out Baby Ruth candy bars, several of which I happily and rapidly ate. Since I had never seen a candy bar, much less eaten so much sugar in one dose, the candy caused me to promptly vomit. Fortunately this proved to only be a temporary problem, and one which my mother fixed once we had reached the American side of the lake by hanging a small sign around my neck with the admonition "Do Not Feed" written on it.

Fortunately the evacuation from the camp, while it took much more time than had been planned, was accomplished without the loss of a single American life. No paratroopers were killed while fighting the

Japanese, although two soldiers lost their lives in the diversionary attack taking place concurrently several miles from the camp.

It is worth noting that the 11th Airborne Division, which distinguished itself in fighting in the Philippines and other Southeast Asian battlefields, regards the rescue operation with enormous pride. The division quickly adopted the motto "The Angels of Los Banos" - a nickname the division carried until it was finally abolished after the Vietnam War. To this day reunions of 11th Airborne Division veterans are always called "Los Banos Nights." The story of the Camp's liberation from behind Japanese lines quickly made newspapers across the United States: no doubt because war news is usually so grim. This was rightfully considered a minor but hugely positive operation that saved rather than took lives. It would probably have been a much larger story except for the fact that the U.S. Marines reached the summit of Mount Suribachi on the island of Iwo Jima on exactly the same day - the 23rd of February 1945 – and the famous picture of the Marines raising the flag on top of Mount Suribachi deservedly caught the public eye.

Once we reached the American side of the lake we were, oddly enough, herded into an empty prison which was the only structure large enough to accommodate the roughly 2,200 internees and their new U.S. Army helpers. We remained there for several days while they sorted out the internees and laid plans for our transport back to the United States. The Army could not do enough for us: the soldiers were obviously appalled by the appearance of many internees, and we were treated with that unique blend of generosity, kindness and organizational skill that is uniquely American.

The last leg of our journey to the United States and freedom was made on a troop ship named the "Admiral Eberly." My memory of that trip basically revolves around eating absolutely endless amounts of food while being thoroughly checked over by Navy doctors and nurses. We were reminded that the war was not yet over by the fact that soon after leaving the Philippines there was a submarine scare which resulted in our ship taking violent evasive maneuvers while we were all restricted to our troop ship bunks. Years later my mother told me that most internees – during this frightening interlude – adopted a rather fatalistic point of view. She said that it seemed only fitting that the Japanese would have one more chance to destroy us all, and the fact that we escaped from the submarine threat was in her eyes just one more manifestation of the incredible prowess of the U.S. military.

The ship docked at San Pedro harbor in California. I remember a band on the dock as the ship was berthed: the band played the "Star Spangled Banner," which I had never heard, but which deeply touched the adult internees, all of whom broke into tears of thanks and appreciation.

We returned to St. Louis Missouri, my mother's ancestral home, where we entered hospitals for a few weeks and were then let loose upon the world.

There are several postscripts to the story of our liberation from Los Banos.

A few days after the rescue mission a unit of the Japanese 10th Infantry Division swept down on the fishing village of Los Banos and slaughtered virtually all of its inhabitants: men, women and children. When American troops subsequently overran the entire area they found the gruesome remains of many hundreds of the people of Los Banos: women tied to trees with their throats cut; men beaten to death; children bayoneted and left to die lingering deaths. This was clearly done as a reprisal for the successful raid – yet no one from the village was involved in any way with the operation, and the hundreds of innocent Filipinos were murdered out of hand. It was later established that Imperial Japanese Army Sergeant Major Konishi, the man who had been the scourge of the internment camp and who had escaped death at the hands of the paratroopers and guerrillas, led this vengeful massacre.

Before their deaths from old age a number of internees from the Los Banos Camp established a scholarship program for students attending a high school at Los Banos. The fund, while small, has enabled a number of young men and women to attend the school, which is affiliated with the University of the Philippines. The fund is also supported by the 11th Airborne Division Association, which regularly contributes money which enables young Filipinos to get an excellent education. This is a gesture that attempts in some small way to make up for the dreadful slaughter that took place early in 1945.

Several months after our liberation, a former internee who had not returned to the United States was playing golf at Manila's premier golf course. He noticed a small group of Japanese prisoners of war at work repairing a road that had been damaged during the fighting in the area of the golf course. The internee happened to look carefully at the faces of each of the Japanese soldiers – and he identified Sergeant Konishi. The sergeant was removed from the work detail, and was sentenced to death at the Japanese War Crimes Trials in Tokyo after the end of World War II. He was executed.

Over the years I read every scrap of information that I could locate on the Los Banos raid. At the time I was simply trying to find out all I could about this almost uniquely successful effort to rescue civilians from behind enemy lines. Little did I know at the time that in 1979 – 1980 I would be heavily involved in planning and executing an attempt to free American hostages being held at the U. S Embassy in Tehran, Iran. The "lessons learned" from the Los Banos raid were very much in my mind as we planned and attempted to execute that sadly ill-fated attempt to rescue our hostages, about which more is written later in this book.

Finally, in closing this account of my life through WWII, I want to pay particular homage to my mother, Eleanor, who managed for 3 ½ extraordinarily difficult years to keep her child alive and healthy in the most difficult circumstances. Her courage and optimism never failed, and her strength in adversity enabled her to bring herself and her child successfully through their time in hell together.

Thanks, Mom, and God Bless you.

2

INDIA AND RETURN TO THE PHILIPPINES

My parents were not only expatriate Americans, they were <u>determined</u> expatriate Americans. Within a year of our return to the United States after our liberation, my father, who worked for what was then the First National City Bank of New York (and is now Citi) accepted an assignment to Calcutta, India, where we arrived early in 1946.

It was impossible to return to the Philippines, particularly to Manila, so soon after the war: the city was in ruins. Calcutta was the next best thing. We spent two years there, which I remember as a very happy time. It did have its moments, however, because when India became independent in August of 1947, the new Muslim state of Pakistan was carved out of what had been British India. Independence brought hideous Hindu - Muslim riots as millions of people had to move between the two countries. Calcutta was one of the major venues for the outbreak of extraordinary violence between the two religious communities, and in 1948 there were periods of violence in the city which came to be known as "the Great Calcutta Killings."

As millions of Hindus and Muslims moved both ways between India and the newly created nation of Pakistan, there were repeated instances of what was called "communal violence" – Muslims killing Hindus and Hindus killing Muslims. We lived in a lovely British style bungalow in one of the better residential areas of Calcutta, yet we woke up one morning to find that our Hindu cook had killed our Muslim bearer – the man responsible for serving meals and in general keeping the house in order. This brought the violence a little too close to home, and after two years in Calcutta my father was offered and accepted another posting to Manila.

Before the terrible Hindu - Muslim bloodbath began we were able to travel extensively in Northern India, and I remember visiting tea estates still run by Englishmen, and going to a number of game preserves in the Indian state of Assam. I learned to speak a little Hindustani from the servants, and in general as a child in the fading days of the British Raj in India I had the fondest memories of the country.

In truth India had worked its way into my blood, and years later at university I studied Hindustani, and majored in Oriental Studies with an emphasis on Afghanistan, India and Pakistan. After I joined CIA I was fortunate in that I was able to utilize this training.

In 1949 we turned up again in the Philippines. While Manila was still being rebuilt, most of the working parts of the city were functioning again. For some odd reason I felt like I was at home. Along with all the other children of American expatriates in Manila I attended the American School. Amazingly, so many of the Americans who had lived through the terrible war years in Japanese internment camps had also returned to the Philippines. In a way it was old home week: I went to school with kids I had been with in Los Banos, and we moved smoothly into the post-war world.

In those years in the Philippines - which lasted roughly from the third through the eighth grades - any number of things happened that in retrospect had a bearing on my later life. When I look back on what I regarded as a perfectly normal life, I now see that it was marked by things that certainly influenced my development and who I grew up to be.

As a practical matter I was an only child. Although my younger brother Chris was born while we were in India, he was seven years younger than I, so we had a completely separate existence: I grew up without a sibling. The next thing was that I saw very little of my mother and father, who were caught up in the Manila business and social whirl to the extent that they were never home in the evenings and were busy with their friends most weekends. I ate my evening meals alone – while being solicitously cared for by a house full of servants. Consequently, I was left to my own devices a great deal of the time. I developed into a voracious reader, and was fortunate in that my father had purchased an entire library of books from a departing expatriate American, a man who had a particular interest in history.

I didn't find any of this to be a problem at the time, and I credit it with enabling me to develop a degree of self-confidence and self-reliance that was perhaps unusual for one my age. At the same time I was able to pursue interests that I might not otherwise have been attracted or exposed to. I certainly had friends from my peer group at school, but I was off on my own a great deal of the time.

Perhaps from a feeling of guilt over general parental inattention, when I was about 11 my father bought me a sailing dinghy. We were members of the Manila Yacht Club, and many were the days after school – and certainly on vacations from school – when I could be found at the Yacht Club sailing by myself. I very nearly wore out that sailing dinghy, and must have capsized it hundreds of times. As I became proficient I graduated from the dinghy to larger sailboats that "the grownups" would let me use. By the time I was 14 I was a very proficient sailor, and was much in demand as crew for adults who were racing their boats. My father later bought a larger boat which I happily sailed alone all over Manila Bay. And, of course, there were opportunities to take my friends sailing with me. I was never interested in team sports such as baseball or soccer, which very much involved most of my peers. Instead I would rather be on the water, and the more stormy the weather and difficult the sailing the better I liked it.

During this period, I became interested in skin diving and scuba diving. This was made possible largely by my friendship with the Parsons family, whose patriarch, "Chick" Parsons, (more about him later) owned a very large motor yacht. Pat Parsons and I were the same age and grade, and he very generously invited me and a number of our mutual friends out on weekend trips on the yacht. Chick was in the vanguard of people using the recently invented Aqua Lung, enjoyed skin diving, and took a very relaxed view of our using his equipment. When we were not diving we would be on water skis and aquaplanes. I was a good swimmer – perhaps because I was so frequently turning myself over in the water while sailing – and I loved every minute of our time swimming in the South China Sea. We would all return from these expeditions badly sunburned, and had the absolute time of our lives.

Like sailing, I found these water sports to be exactly what I most liked to do. I always found the ever present threat of sharks to be something of a challenge. I was no fool, and would get the hell out of the water anytime someone said "shark," but I certainly had no fear of the possibility that they were swimming exactly where we were. Like sailing, skin diving allowed me to develop considerable self-confidence and a degree of expertise.

Chick Parsons, whom we all called "Uncle Chick," was an authentic hero of World War II in the Philippines. He was assigned to General MacArthur's staff in Australia, made repeated trips by submarine to the Philippines, contacting guerrillas and providing weapons, radios, funds, cryptographic equipment and other items which enabled guerrilla units to effectively fight the Japanese. His stories of just a few of his missions to the Philippines were absolutely enthralling to his audience of youngsters. Without meaning to Chick was teaching us a great deal about how to supply and support a major guerrilla war. To say the least he was my childhood hero, and I will admit that in later years I consciously wanted to emulate his extraordinary courage and intelligence. I could not, but it certainly was a goal that subconsciously drove me through the years.

During this period of my life in the Philippines, I was privileged on a number of occasions to listen to Americans who had waged guerrilla war against the Japanese Imperial Army. They told of their mistakes and their hardships, their victories and their strategies. All in all it was an education in running guerrilla warfare. Little did I realize that many years later, when I was assigned by CIA to Pakistan to initiate and build up a full-blown guerrilla war against the Soviets, the lessons I learned at the knees of Uncle Chick and other hard-bitten guerrilla veterans would do much to guide me in planning and executing what I have come to call the First Afghan War – a guerrilla war that eventually ejected the Soviets from Afghanistan.

Oddly enough another lifelong interest of mine was born in the ruins of our house in Manila, which had been totally destroyed in the fighting for the city. Before the house was rebuilt I was plowing around in the wreckage and found a pistol, a rusty and beat up "Liberator", that was a leftover from the war. I have ever since loved and collected American military firearms.

This fairly idyllic lifestyle came to a crashing end when I completed the eighth grade. For reasons unknown to me, my parents decided that I should go to the United States to prep school. One of my very best chums, Blayney Colmore, came from a family that had for generations attended Kent School in Kent, Connecticut, and Blayney and I were to be sent off to New England. This without consultation with me, and I was far too young and too obedient a boy to object. I actually wanted to go away to school in the Philippines – to Brent School, another Episcopal boarding school that, like Kent, had been established early in the 1900's.

In 1954, Kent was an all-boys school where the inmates led a fairly monastic life. The academic load was a stringent one, and the fundamental premise seemed to be – <u>a la</u> U.S. Marine boot camp – that young boys should be broken down first and then built up to be men. Not a bad philosophy, all things considered. Kent was the first time that I had ever lived in the United States, so I had a crash course in America. The school also operated on the philosophy that we all had jobs to do, starting with the menial business of cleaning the bathrooms, doing the dishes in the dining hall kitchen, breaking up ice on the sidewalks and the myriad other tasks needed to keep the place going. This was part of making men out of us. We younger boys of course drew the grubbiest and unpleasant tasks, and the burden got lighter as one marched up over the years to become Sixth Formers – seniors, who, in effect, basically ran much of the School.

I found my classmates to be an extraordinarily fine bunch of young men. While I had never had to lift a finger in my servant-rich life up to this point, I had no problem going with the flow. One thing that bothered me about Kent was that boys older than I were automatically granted privileges and immunities based simply on their age. But, we were told, all good things would come to us as we too grew older: suffering would eventually have its rewards As a kid from the tropics I also found New England's frigid winters to be a huge pain in the ass.

At Kent everyone was required to engage in team sports: it was almost a religious exercise. In my case, this meant football in the Fall and rowing in the Spring. I had never seen an American football, much less a football game, and I remember my astonishment in discovering that the "ball" in football had pointed ends. To my surprise however, I found that I enjoyed both sports. Since I was big for my age, I drew the position of right tackle on my intramural team, which suited me perfectly, since I didn't have to bother to learn the complex plays that were devised by our coaches: my job was simply to take down the boy opposite me on the line of scrimmage, and/or to tackle the quarterback or whoever else on the opposing team had the ball. Very straightforward, and rather fun.

While I only did two years at Kent, many years later I was reunited with my classmates and welcomed back by them as though I had done a full four years at the school. I consider myself to be truly fortunate to have made friends with my classmates, and am very proud that they have done me the honor of including me in their number. They were outstanding boys and grew, unsurprisingly, into outstanding men. Not only did they welcome me with open arms, but the Kent Alumni Council made me a member of a society of Kent graduates who had rendered outstanding service. I received a fair number of medals and awards while at CIA, but this honor is the most important to me.

On my return to the Philippines for summer vacation after my second year at Kent, I discovered that my parents had embarked on a remarkable entrepreneurial adventure. My father had resigned from the bank, and he and my mother, who was the brains behind the endeavor, were attempting to establish a huge solar salt and the fish pond operation at a remote location called Tambac Bay about 5 hours by road from Manila. The project was well underway, with huge bulldozers moving vast amounts of dirt to create ponds in which salt would be produced in the dry season and fish raised in the wet. This was a massive undertaking, complicated by the fact that it was necessary to employ several hundred local Filipinos and come to grips with communist bandits who were operating in the neighborhood. I threw myself into the role of construction supervisor and "liaison officer" with the local villagers. At the ripe old age of 15 I found that I was doing a man's job – and I loved every minute of it. Tambac Bay was also near the "1000 Islands," a skin and scuba diving paradise. Pure heaven.

I was honestly enthusiastic about the project, and I wanted to remain as close to it as a possible. This gave me the opportunity to tell my parents that I would prefer to go to a boarding school in Baguio, just a few hours from Tambac, and thus be able to frequently visit the project site and continue to participate in the creation of what would eventually grow to be a very large and successful endeavor. They acquiesced, and at the end of the summer I marched off to Brent School in Baguio City, Philippines – a mere 5 hours away.

Brent was a much smaller school than Kent, was co-ed, and was attended by American kids from all over the Far East. I thrived in my new school environment, was very involved in student government, and look back on my two years at school there with great fondness. My graduating class was all of 15 people, and I have been in contact with alumni from the school ever since.

In retrospect, having attended both Kent and Brent provided me with an extraordinarily good education, and remarkable opportunities to mature and expand my horizons. I could not have been given a better high school experience. That, and my exposure to the building of Tambac Bay, was, I believe, the single most important educational experience of my life.

My thinking as I was preparing to graduate from high school was that I should go to university and study subjects that would prepare me to return to the Philippines to help operate the Tambac Bay project. For that reason I was accepted at Cornell University in the College of Agriculture.

Cornell was a rude awakening. For some reason I had forgotten the dreadful winters in the northeastern United States. I also discovered that agriculture, with its heavy load of chemistry, biology, botany, geology and agricultural economics, was definitely not my forte. More to the point, I found I had no interest in those academic disciplines, and by the end of my first semester I had switched to the Liberal Arts College. While unsure what specific degree studies I would pursue at Cornell, the one thing I knew for certain was that I would obtain a U.S. Army commission through Cornell's ROTC program. Here was the first stirring of a desire to serve my country: I did not fully realize it at the time, but I was already gravitating towards a career in government service. I certainly did not consciously remember that young paratrooper who helped carry me to freedom from the Japanese internment camp, but I did recognize that in some way I wanted to spend my life serving my country. I realize that such a statement may sound antique and naïve in the early 21st century, but it seemed to me to be the logical outcome of the years leading up to university. It would take several more years, and some serious hiccups in my college career, for me to arrive at my ultimate destination – working for CIA's National Clandestine Service.

When I returned to the Philippines after my first year at Cornell I discovered that things had gone very badly for my parents as regards Tambac Bay: to my absolute astonishment I found that my father had lost the project, and was now financially ruined. The project had so much potential, but was under-financed, and he did not have any financial control, which made the venture vulnerable. Dad always believed that it was effectively stolen from him. Since the Filipino businessmen responsible for this sad state of affairs were well connected in the Philippine government, lawsuits brought by my father to regain his interests were mysteriously never heard in the court room, and decades of legal effort by him came to nothing.

It was obviously financially impossible for me to return to Cornell, and when my father and mother moved to Hawaii where he took a job with a bank in Honolulu, I followed along and went to work to help contribute to the family finances. I put off returning to university for two years, at the end of which time I decided that I had to get back into school on my own dime. I had also decided that I wanted to major in political science with a strong emphasis on Asia.

I flew to California and interviewed with the University of California at Berkeley, which had a very strong Asian Studies program. I found that in order to qualify as a state resident – and attend Berkeley at in-state tuition rates – I had to spend a year living and working in California, which meant that I would "waste" one more year. I will admit that as a product of an East Coast education I was convinced that, with the exception to Berkeley and Stanford, all education in the

United States ended at the western edge of Ithaca, New York. So much for the arrogance of youth.

Due to a very fortunate combination of circumstances I wound up in Tucson, Arizona, where I discovered that the University of Arizona not only had excellent Oriental Studies and Political Science programs, but that the school would facilitate my admission at in-state tuition rates. I was initially puzzled why Arizona would have such an excellent Asian area studies program: the answer, of course, was simple. Professors with health problems and degrees from Ivy League schools had come to Arizona for the dry climate, and the University was prepared to fund very strong Departments in my area of interest.

Once I had organized my schooling I found a full time job as an announcer at a radio station in Tucson. The pay was pathetically low, but sufficient to enable me to attend school – with the added benefit that the radio station would allow me to arrange my working hours to accommodate my academic course load. The result was that I worked 40 hour weeks at the radio station, and attended the university full time, for the next four years. At the end of that time I had attained a B.A. degree (in the University's Honors program) and an M.A. - both degrees in Oriental Studies/Political Science. Arizona was and is a fine university, and I owe it and a number of friends in Arizona my deepest thanks for having made possible my attending the school. Financial pressures eased considerably in my Master's year as I received a scholarship that paid my tuition and provided a living stipend. I felt then as though I was rolling in money, and I couldn't believe that someone would actually pay me to go to school.

While I was at University it was very clear to me that my career would have to be in some form of government service – what that service might be hung in the air. I briefly digressed from my regular program when I was persuaded by Bob Andrews, a fellow student and a much admired friend who was beginning his career in the law, to apply for and attend the University's Law School. I did this, and lasted exactly one semester. I found the law intellectually interesting and certainly challenging, but I learned that I did not want to become a lawyer, so I switched back into Oriental Studies and used the law courses as elective credits. I've always been grateful for having done that semester since it taught me a good deal about oral arguments and crisp, clear professional writing; skills which would serve me well in CIA. And I learned that there are good, bad and indifferent lawyers.

The only other digression, and one that I did <u>not</u> make, was the possibility of going into a career in academia. Out of the blue I was offered a fellowship to attend the Woodrow Wilson School at Princeton University to work towards a Ph.D\ At the time this seemed a very tempting offer, but I knew that in my heart of hearts the academic world would not provide me with a sort of hands-on, "in the field" work that I wanted to do. In retrospect that was one of the easier decisions I ever had to make in choosing my career path.

Sometime early in my senior year CIA made its appearance in my life: a CIA recruiter turned up on campus and I interviewed with him. He said almost nothing about what work at CIA would entail – other than that it would probably be overseas. I had, of course, no knowledge of what CIA actually did, but the interview did suggest that CIA might be a gateway into an exciting career in service to my country. As a result of this interview I took a day's worth of written tests and submitted an enormously long and very detailed application. I was told not to hold my breath while waiting for a response, as, said the recruiter, the wheels grind exceeding slow. He had that right, for I heard nothing from the Agency for almost a year. I assumed, therefore, that the Agency had no interest in me, and as I got closer to graduation the need to find employment grew exponentially. I dismissed applying to the State Department, as I had relatives in the Foreign Service who had candidly painted a fairly unflattering picture of a career in that service. I <u>was</u> interested in the Marine Corps, and when Marine recruiters came to campus in search of officer candidates I met with them and submitted an application for Marine Corps Officer Candidate School. The Marines were a great deal more responsive than CIA was, and my application actually got to the point where I would have to sign up and commit to at least starting a career as a Marine officer. The Vietnam war had not yet grown to anywhere near the full catastrophe that it turned out to be, but I was fairly certain that the war would expand and that the Marines would be in it. While I was opposed to the war on the basis that it could not possibly be won, I was quite prepared to serve should the Marine Corps become involved.

Just prior to signing up with the Marine Corps, CIA came to life. I was flown to Washington where I had several interviews and a polygraph "examination." I told my CIA recruiter contact of my moving towards the Marines, and as a former Marine he certainly understood my motivation. But, said he, CIA could make far better use of my area training and language skills then could the Corps. He also said that I would find more than enough excitement in a CIA career. Apparently he lit a fire under the recruiting people at CIA Headquarters, and I was asked to return to Washington where I was offered a job at CIA, which I accepted with alacrity.

3

ENTERING CIA

When I entered on duty at CIA in the early summer of 1966 we were at the height of the Cold War. The Cuban missile crisis was just a few years behind us; we had lost President Kennedy; and the war in Vietnam – and our involvement in it – was beginning to heat up. It would have been inconceivable at the time to think that the Soviet Union would collapse less than three decades later. CIA at that time was very much involved, with varying degrees of success, in fighting a secret war with the Soviets. It was a shooting war by proxy in places like the Congo, a quiet war for military and political intelligence, and a struggle for political influence around much of the rest of the world.

Few Americans, even those who lived through the Cold War years, appreciate the fact that the United States had in fact placed its national existence on the line as we and the Soviets glowered at each other, each side armed to the teeth with nuclear weapons. America did this to keep the Soviets out of Europe and, to a lesser degree, out of much of the Third World.

In a way, the world was much simpler then: we knew exactly who our enemies were: principally the Soviets and to a lesser extent the Chinese. International terrorism and radical Islam had not yet raised their fearsome and ugly heads.

I joined CIA as a Career Trainee (CT), the Agency's primary way to secure an input of career junior officers who would grow over the years to become the next generation of the Agency's leaders. Even with the Agency growing in size in response to its increased commitment to counterinsurgency – which at the time meant fighting the Vietcong guerrillas in South Vietnam – its primary business was espionage. I want to make clear that I didn't join just CIA ... I joined CIA's Clandestine Service - which is now called the National Clandestine Service, hereafter referred to as the NCS.

The word "espionage" merits a definition: it is obtaining secret information (intelligence) from human sources in target governments on <u>the plans and intentions</u> of those governments. This includes information on their military capabilities; their economies; and on their political activities, both internal and external. "Espionage" is the three dollar word for spying: without question the world's second oldest profession.

A few more definitions: "Intelligence": pure and simple, intelligence is <u>information</u>. Everyone is in the intelligence business, from reading the daily newspaper to making stock picks to checking out schools for one's children ... every one of us collects and uses intelligence in the course of our daily lives. In the "intelligence business" the information collected is both "open source" (i.e., information available in newspapers, books, television and radio and academic publications) and "secret source." All intelligence agencies collect and analyze "open source" information. In addition, world-class intelligence services attempt to collect information that is <u>not</u> in the public domain. The point of the exercise being to meld open source information with secret information in order to get the best possible picture of what is happening on a given subject or country.

CIA, like the Department of State, is in the "foreign intelligence" business. Which is a very specific term that means the Agency does not collect intelligence information concerning the United States: it is expressly forbidden by law to do that. Put another way, the Agency collects intelligence only on foreign countries and foreigners.

Unlike the FBI, CIA does not call its National Clandestine Service officers "agents": that term is used by CIA exclusively to refer to foreigners with whom we have clandestine intelligence relationships. They are the spies. We refer to our agents as sources or assets, and every agent is a "case." Our people are called "Operations Officers," for which the shorthand term is "Case Officers." CIA's NCS Case Officers recruit, run, and handle agents.

The small group of young men (and a few women) that I joined the Agency with was, certainly in our estimation at least, a bright bunch. Everyone had a Masters or Law degree, and most had at least a rudimentary grounding in one or more foreign languages. We came from all over the country – not just the Ivy League, as is frequently alleged. I later learned that we all fit into a carefully defined "psychological box" that the Agency had over the years developed to identify potentially successful operations officers. That said, it certainly seemed to us that we were a group with some wildly different personalities and experiences.

What we had in common was a desire to make a career out of the intelligence business, and, more specifically, in the clandestine intelligence operations business – about which we knew absolutely nothing. I emphasize the word "career." None of us joined CIA as a lark, or as a stepping stone to some other career: we planned to remain in the Agency for our entire working lives. I suspect that as much as ninety percent of us served full careers in the Agency – an incredible retention rate for any organization.

We had a high work ethic. We had been warned by our recruiters that a career in the Agency would be very demanding, and called for a much higher level of personal commitment than was the case in either the private sector or in other government agencies. Most of us regarded that truth as a welcome challenge. Those of us who did not – and there were very few such people – soon dropped out or moved to less demanding jobs in the Agency.

We were told that we were the most carefully selected group of entry-level people in the US government – with the exception of the then-budding astronaut program. The interview process and psychological testing alone were comprehensive; as were the medical examinations and the security checks that were run on each of us. Unlike the State Department, in choosing its junior officer trainees the Agency did not formally test us for our current affairs or area knowledge: the Agency assumed that since we had all done well in University we had an adequate grounding in our respective fields. Since no University gave degrees in espionage, the Agency assumed that we were blank slates on which it would write our professional knowledge and qualifications. This comprehensive process resulted in the lengthy delays in hearing back from the Agency while we were in the pre-employment application process.

As part of the pre-employment process we all had to go through polygraph examinations – the infamous lie detector. The polygraph focused on our personal honesty and integrity, and on the question of contacts with foreign nationals. In the latter case the questioning is designed to find out if an individual candidate is actually being directed by, and is under the control of, a hostile intelligence service seeking to penetrate the Agency - or whether an individual might be subject to pressures by a foreign intelligence service.

While a useful tool, the polygraph can be hideously wrong. For example the one question in my pre-employment polygraph examination that became an "issue" was that of my <u>name</u>: when I was asked if I was using my real name, the polygraph needle went off the chart. To say the least this bothered the polygraph operator. In the end we worked it out because the reason I had a physiological reaction to the question was that I had legally changed my surname from that of my biological father to that of my stepfather.

I, like my fellow case officers, also was subject to polygraphs that were administered on several occasions throughout my career in the Service. The focus of these "re-investigations" was always and <u>only</u> on issues of counterintelligence, essentially to verify that I continued to meet the security requirements of the job. Knowing that there would be periodic re-investigations was enough to keep most people on the straight and narrow when it came to observing security requirements. Those initial briefings informed us that Agency employees are targets of very real and serious programs by foreign intelligence services to penetrate the organization. The maximum threat was and is represented by the Russians and the Chinese, both of whom have large and active programs to recruit people inside CIA. They have accomplished this by spotting CIA employees who for one reason or other, usually financial, have elected to spy for them. The Aldrich Ames case is the most widely known incident in this running battle against hostile attempts to penetrate the Agency. Nor are such attempts limited to governments like those of Russia and China; the Israelis are known to have worked to recruit spies inside the Agency.

In recalling my earliest impressions of the Agency when I entered on duty I think the biggest surprise was the scope of activities the Agency was involved in, and how many people were devoted to those activities. Given that we were exposed to most of the key elements of the entire Agency, it was a rare day that I did not go home astonished at both the tasks borne by the Agency and its capabilities. The impression that somewhere inside the Agency there were people with extraordinary capabilities on almost any given intelligence subject; and people who could and would support the most arcane intelligence activities, remained with me throughout my career.

The need for security was a fact of life that I discovered immediately. This covered everything from the secure storage of classified materials, to protecting our covers, to "fencing off" operational matters or intelligence products through a procedure called compartmentation – the process of limiting knowledge to those who need it. The principle of "need to know" permeated every level and every sphere of Agency activities. This is not a question of trust: it is that sensitive information is kept secret by reducing the number of people who are exposed to it. Since virtually everything that the Agency does or is involved in is classified, this means that informal conversations between Agency employees are usually restricted to family matters, football games, or articles in the day's newspapers.

We were bred <u>not</u> to have security violations. This meant everything from being sure that your work materials were properly "secured" (we all developed an almost pathological fear of leaving our office safes open at night) to not telling your spouse what you were doing. And protecting one's cover – which most NCS CT's were under – became almost a holy ritual. Some young officers never got the hang of this, and were perpetually guilty of some security violation or other. A small number of people found this process untenable and left the Agency.

TRAINING

The Agency knocked itself out to give National Clandestine Service CTs the training we needed. Our training program was very nearly 2 years long, and alternated between formal courses and brief periods on "interim assignments" at Headquarters. An interim assignment, where one is normally assigned to a specific branch or office, provides the opportunity to see just how that unit - and the Agency in general – does its business. It was a good dose of reality while we were busily involved in case officer training where everything was "notional."

At the beginning of the training period weeks were spent familiarizing us with how the Agency was set up and who did what; a real eye-opener. Because we were CT's, all of the major offices across the full spectrum of the Agency sent people to brief us on what they were doing – their role in the entire process of intelligence gathering and the production of "finished intelligence": the Agency's final "product." We had short courses in everything from how to present briefings to how the names of foreigners were indexed in the Agency's enormous databases. We learned how to write intelligence reports, both analytical pieces - "finished intelligence" - and reports based on information given to us by (notional) agent sources: so-called "raw intelligence." After this introductory period we were sent off to the "Farm" to receive our formal training in how to be operations officers: what we jokingly called "spy school."

The Farm was a tiresome drive from Headquarters, and the Operations Course lasted, as I recall, for almost 5 months. This meant that we had to leave our Washington homes late Sunday afternoons, and be gone until late Friday afternoon or evening. This was difficult for those of us who had spouses and in many instances young children.

The "Ops Course" is and was taught by Case Officers who were on rotation from Headquarters or overseas assignments. This made sense since we were taught by people who had spent years doing the jobs that we were being trained to fill. With few exceptions, the quality of our instructors was very high. The course was a mixture of instruction on almost every conceivable subject that might have a bearing on the intelligence "process," and an introduction to – and training in – the fundamentals of a Case Officer's job overseas: recruiting and running agents. This is what CIA's Founding Director, Allen Dulles, called "the craft of intelligence," and what all operations officers refer to as "tradecraft."

With our training officers we simulated the process of recruiting new agents, a complicated and difficult process. Agents, by definition, are betraying their countries, and if discovered suffer huge penalties – up to and including execution. Since targets for recruitment are very well aware of this, it is very difficult to identify and recruit agents.

There is an "agent recruitment cycle," a process by which agent prospects are identified; a relationship developed; a determination made of the potential agent in terms of his access to information of value; and an assessment of how the individual might be persuaded to agree to a clandestine relationship. The bottom line is that agent recruitments are based on ideological grounds, financial remuneration, or both. Recruitments are never made, despite Hollywood assertions otherwise, on the basis of blackmail. One of the guiding principles in the recruitment process is avoiding "blowback": one does not want to make a pitch to a recruitment target that results in the target making a scene and exposing the recruiting officer.

Recruiting agents is the lifeblood of the Service, and is probably the most difficult of all the skills that case officers should have. Relatively few officers are actually good at it, and I think a majority of officers, while they may go through the motions, basically do not engage in agent recruitments. While the service rewards excellent recruiters, there certainly are not enough of them. For even very talented recruiting officers it is probably fair to say that if one recruits three or four <u>high value agents</u> in one's career one has done very well. While most officers may make a series of low-level recruitments over their careers, most will not hit home runs when it comes to recruiting valuable and unique "assets" (another term for agents.)

The Agency has struggled with this fact since its inception – as I believe all other intelligence services have. It is just plain difficult to identify and recruit spies.

We were also trained in the "tradecraft" of clandestine agent operations: basically how to keep the relationship between agent and case officer clandestine. Classical espionage tradecraft covers a wide variety of subjects, perhaps the most important of which was protecting one's agents by keeping contact between the Case Officer and agent secret. The rule was – and is – that contact between Case Officers and agents, while necessary, had to be accomplished in a manner that would not be seen by a hostile counter–intelligence service. Since virtually all other intelligence services are deemed hostile, and all operations are run on the assumption that we are always under surveillance by <u>someone</u>, this meant that our agent communications had to be invisible. While today's electronic world has made secure "impersonal" contact much easier – both in terms of passing intelligence from agent to case officer, and in providing guidance from the case officer to the agent – techniques developed long ago by espionage services are still required.

One example: if it is necessary to pass equipment to an agent one does not ring him up, meet him at a bar, and hand him a package full of compromising agent communications equipment, money or other "spy" items. To do this securely one frequently resorts to use of a "dead drop," where the Case Officer leaves the package at some safe location and departs the area. Sometime later the agent comes by and retrieves the package: there is no direct contact between either person. This sounds simple and straightforward, but it seldom is, since where one leaves the package so that it will not be found or picked up by either hostile counter-intelligence or just innocent third parties can be a very difficult issue. I have literally spent days searching for and identifying "secure" places where I could leave packages of various sizes for my agents to subsequently retrieve. This is particularly difficult to accomplish in Third World countries where there is normally a large population busily engaged in picking up anything that might be of value.

Tradecraft covers the nuts and bolts of maintaining contacts with agents. It also involves such arcane matters as conducting and detecting surveillance; the use of secret writing; clandestine radio contacts; signals to agents (for example, to trigger a dead drop) and myriad other subjects associated with keeping an agent safe while obtaining intelligence information from him.

Nothing, of course, ever goes by the book, and very often the most mundane tradecraft issues are complicated by either the local environment or by the odd behavior of agents. I soon figured out that the most important thing that any case officer must have is a huge dose of common sense. It was interesting to see which of our group had the requisite common sense to become "streetwise." Our instructors made a point, once they believed we had grasped the fundamentals of tradecraft, to throw us curveballs, usually by the instructor playing the role of an agent performing some weird act that would require us to amend carefully laid plans. As is the case in the real world of clandestine operations, the unexpected is the norm, and the case officer had better be prepared to roll with the punch and still accomplish whatever his task might be.

I was told by my recruiting officer, a retired National Clandestine Service officer with a wealth of experience, that what made a great operations officer was common sense coupled with a sponge-like ability to soak up all manner of information and trivia that could at some point be used in the field. He was dead right. Truly great case officers are people with imaginative minds, quick reactions and enormous "situational awareness." Added to this is a requirement for considerable social skills and an ability to assess people well. Successful case officers are usually extroverts – but sensible ones. In my mind the really excellent operations officer is something of a Renaissance man or woman. In addition to practicing excellent tradecraft skills and working hard at recruiting new agents, the superior officer needs to have very broad interests which enable him or her to deal with wildly varying types of people. One never knows what bit of knowledge or area of interest will turn out to be germane to conducting intelligence operations. I invariably found that our best officers were inveterate readers with very high levels of curiosity. People with narrow vision and mindsets do not make outstanding operations officers.

This brings me to the subject of "management skills." As is the case in most companies in the private sector, as our officers grow they find themselves in charge of other people. At first this may mean supervising a handful of subordinates, but for officers who are moving up the promotion ladder their management responsibilities grow over the years. Whether one is managing a large Headquarters component or a Station, managing people well is a critical skill. And it is not one that is formally taught. We basically learn management by <u>managing</u>, a process that is not always successful. If an officer is fortunate enough at several points in his or her career to work for truly gifted managers, one learns these skills by <u>being managed</u>. If, on the other hand, one does not have effective management role models and mentors along the way, learning how to manage can be a little rough.

My own philosophy – and I was fortunate to work for several role models and mentors who were highly competent managers – is that management boils down to two things: <u>leading people,</u> and using personnel resources to take the best advantage of their skills - while recognizing their limitations. I am also convinced that in the NCS good managers are people who have developed a gut instinct on how to get the best out of their people.

The Service's workforce is a fairly disciplined one – certainly not like the military, but probably as much or more disciplined than in private industry. When one is stuck with a poor manager one just has to soldier on and do the best one can, and I certainly had my fair share of poor managers. But I also had some brilliant ones. As no doubt is the case elsewhere, I often found that senior managers who considered themselves to be absolutely brilliant with regard to their managerial skills were actually largely incompetent. Such people were usually arrogant, humorless, and hugely confident in their own abilities. A senior Agency officer once told me that a man's competence varied inversely to his degree of pomposity.

I also found that one key to effective management is a high degree of collegiality. We are fortunate that in the Service people <u>want</u> to get things done, and the more difficult the challenge, and the more we work under the pressures of one crisis or another, the more productive the given organization will be. The downside to this is that people wear themselves out, and the skilled manager has to learn when and how to give his subordinates some relief. No one can work at 100 percent indefinitely, and the espionage business has more than its share of protracted crises.

In my day clandestine operations training was accompanied by extensive training in "paramilitary operations." This course was over four months long, and consisted of training officers in various military fundamentals. The training covered everything from the use of small arms; explosives; small unit tactics; jungle warfare and parachute jumping. In many ways this training mirrored that given to OSS operatives in World War II before they were parachuted into Occupied

Europe. Some wags in the course always came up with a comment to the effect that "Europe has been liberated, so why are we being taught all this stuff."

I was not one of those who considered the course to be irrelevant to our careers in espionage. But, in fact, I used lessons and techniques that I learned in the paramilitary course several times in my career. In effect, it was just one component, and a very useful one, in that extensive catalog of knowledge that we picked up during training and learned in subsequent years.

I also found the paramilitary course of value since it taught us a lot about each other. Classroom and "on the street" training in the dark arts of espionage enabled us to get a pretty good reading on each other. Going through parachute jump school and jungle training, however, also provided an excellent window to how each individual thought and behaved. It was a truism that the most "macho" and pompous of our number were the least anxious to get out of perfectly good airplanes at 1000 feet. I was way ahead as regards the jump training because while at Cornell a fraternity brother of mine and I established the (completely unsanctioned by the University) "Cornell Skydiving Club." I had done about 25 jumps before I left Cornell, and the military style of parachute jumping that we went through in the Agency was a snap.

In my case my paramilitary training was an outstanding background for my job years later when I was called upon to help start and then run a major war against the Soviets in Afghanistan. A few more thoughts before moving on:

CIA, and more specifically the NCS, has frequently been pilloried in the press and by Congress. Certainly the Agency has had its failures. It is also been very badly handled by some Presidents, by some Directors, and more than occasionally by Congress. There are times when all this criticism, bad press and mishandling have had an adverse effect on morale. This is particularly the case because CIA people believe that they and their Agency are on the whole doing more than a good job; which they are.

A clutch of almost professionally anti-CIA voices exist in America: the political Left wing, in and out of Congress; the New York Times (which we frequently and only half-jokingly call an anti-American newspaper) are only two of the most vociferous critics. Failures, real and imagined, are trumpeted. President Jimmy Carter, when he came to office, would probably have abolished CIA if Congress had allowed him to do so. Carter's ignorance of how to deal with foreign affairs was breathtaking, and the Iran crisis gave CIA the opportunity to demonstrate just how valuable a tool it is.

The fact is: CIA works only for the President, and is part of his National Security "team." Some Presidents have made full and competent use of the enormous asset that CIA is for them. Others have not. Even more interesting is the situation where one President, in this case, George Bush 2, established ground rules and tasking for the Agency that his successor, Barack Obama, called illegal and repugnant. In this instance Bush 2 directed and approved the NCS's use of harsh interrogations of known terrorists; Obama called a halt to such interrogations and opted to kill known terrorists by remote control, firing rockets from drone aircraft. Take your pick.

It is a truth that when all is said and done Presidents alone make foreign policy. In really crucial decisions regarding foreign policy, advice from the State Department, from CIA and from the Department of Defense is accepted only if it matches what the President wants to do. The Department of State no more makes foreign policy than does the Boy Scouts of America. Presidents do what they want: if intelligence supports a given policy, all the better. If it does not, ignore it. I am not being cynical ... this is actually the way the most important foreign-policy decisions are made. Put another way, the entire national security apparatus, including intelligence, is and must be absolutely responsive to whatever plans or policies a President puts in place. Period.

As a wise former Secretary of State once told me, "the President calls the shots ... and we are just along for the ride".

It can be a very interesting and exciting ride.

4

BACK TO SOUTH ASIA

After almost 2 years of training I was off to my first posting – a major city in South Asia - where I arrived in 1968, just short of my 28th birthday.

I knew that my first posting would be where I would learn my trade, and for some obscure and undefined reason I felt this would be an ideal place to do that. My family and I arrived in the late spring of 1968, and we spent almost two years there before moving to another South Asian city.

My first wife, Susan, took to the assignment like a duck to water: no small trick for a young woman from the wilds of Indiana. Our first son, Colin, was about 18 months old, and he was put immediately into the care of a wonderful young woman named Magdalena, who was our Christian convent–trained "nanny." Magdalena stayed with us for our entire time in the subcontinent, and came with us all the way through our time in Iran. We had our second child, Guy. There were excellent medical facilities and as Susan later said, having a baby there was infinitely easier than in the United States. Between a house full of servants and Magdalena, the burdens of having a new baby and child going on two years of age were greatly reduced for her.

As I had expected, I very much enjoyed this tour. The work was interesting and, for a first-tour young officer, challenging. I had chosen the NCS Division that deals with the Near East and South Asia because I felt that more was going on there than in any number of more comfortable and healthy places. With one exception, I spent my entire overseas career in this Division and never regretted one minute of it. As I frequently joked, I only had one assignment in a country where one could safely drink the tap water.

As a new and very junior officer I had to put to use all of the things that we had been trained in for so long. In many ways my first months were a very humbling experience: it's all very well to do a good job in a training situation. but when one hits "the field" reality takes over and one realizes that this is "the real stuff."

As was the case in almost all of our field stations our primary targets were Soviet and Soviet Bloc diplomats. It was in our national interest to be aware of what the local Communists were up to as we regarded the country as an important and democratic state in the community of nations, and we knew that the Soviets were funding and guiding the local Communist Party.

I was of course consumed with chasing potential agents from within the Soviet and Eastern European community which, unlike Westerners, was closely monitored by their internal security people. Most Soviets lived in controlled housing where they were more easily monitored by their KGB keepers. I developed a friendship with a very nice young Soviet named Yuri, and we saw a good deal of each other socially. Yuri was a KGB officer under cover as a diplomat in the Soviet Consulate. Yuri, of course, was equally interested in me as a potential recruitment target. I'll never forget an amusing incident where Yuri invited my wife and me to their apartment for dinner. We knew that Yuri and his family lived in an apartment block that was exclusively for Soviet Consulate personnel, but the dinner was held at an apartment away from where all the Soviets lived. Yuri and his wife pretended that this was their home, when in fact it was an empty apartment set up exclusively for the purpose of attempting to show that Soviets too lived "normal" lives. The pretense was a hollow one, as, for example, there was no family bric-a-brac in the place, the bathroom cabinet was empty, and there were literally no signs that someone actually live there. The dinner was catered. We went along with the pretense and admired the furnishings and their choice of draperies. This was very common for Soviets abroad: on the one hand they lived under very controlled circumstances, yet they went some pains to pretend that they did not. Only KGB officers were allowed to have contact with Westerners, although that contact was closely monitored by the KGB "residentura" – the Soviet term for a KGB Station.

The Soviet name for what we call a Chief of Station (COS) is "Rezident." Many years later, when in Pakistan running the insurgency against the Soviets in Afghanistan, Yuri turned up as the KGB Rezident. That was not a coincidence, and Yuri and I met several times in Islamabad reminiscing about "the old days." As the KGB was fully aware that I was a CIA officer, Yuri had clearly been sent to Pakistan on the basis of our social/professional relationship.

I set myself a rather ambitious schedule for my personal development. My first task was to familiarize myself with the city so that I would be able to operate without blundering into trouble.

People from "world power" countries such as the Soviet Union (and its surrogates from Eastern Europe) the United States, Britain, etc., could expect to be fairly closely monitored – as indeed was the case. By and large one came to accept this suspicion of foreigners, but it did mean that one could expect to be under official scrutiny at all times. Security manpower was cheap; the mechanisms were in place, so business continued as usual. Certainly foreigners did not receive the kind of attention they did while living in the Soviet Union and in communist bloc countries, but everyone correctly assumed that their activities were being monitored.

The second task that I assigned myself was to review all of the cases that I had "inherited" to make sure that they were being managed with the maximum attention to tradecraft, and to estimate how I could improve both the tradecraft aspects of the case, if needed, and its intelligence production. In other words, I set out to determine if there were any weaknesses that I could fix and/or improvements that I could make. Since I had been preceded by a very competent officer I found no "holes" that I needed to plug. Reassured, I vowed to run every operation that I was involved in as well as I could possibly manage. This goes back to my initial comments on the importance of safeguarding agents. Now that I was actually "handling" agent assets whose lives were very much in my hands, I was deadly serious about protecting them. This is a common trait among all case officers: one cannot be flippant or careless in dealing with agents. These are real people with real lives who for one reason or other are cooperating with us. They are owed the highest standard of operational "care." If an operation is compromised not only is the agent (or agents, if several are involved in one case) at risk, but the ensuing flap can cause great embarrassment to the United States Government. For this reason the most junior case officer abroad has in his hands a grave responsibility for avoiding the exposure of sources and methods. No Foreign Service Officer operates under such conditions: huge responsibilities are placed on our most junior officers immediately on their arrival in the field – a situation that never ends so long as one is actually running agents.

This is so important that I want to restate it: even the most mundane of our agent operations involves real people who will pay real penalties if they are exposed. Add to this the responsibility of not embarrassing the US Government – with possible very adverse results to our presence in a country. These twin responsibilities should and do weigh heavily on a case officers mind. Stress is guaranteed, and that stress never ends so long as one is directly engaged in agent operations.

I was hugely fortunate in that in my first assignment, a man older than I was with years of experience overseas, was my boss. George was very seized by the fact that one of his primary responsibilities was mentoring this new young case officer, and I learned a great deal from George as the months rolled by. A more decent and helpful man could not have been found, and George was a friend, a counselor and an excellent supervisor. I found it easy to work with him and had enormous respect for his talents and knowledge. It is not always the case that a first-tour officer winds up working for a man who actually is willing to take the time to provide advice and the occasional course-correction that all young case officers require. George affected an easy going and laid-back approach to life but, like most of us, inside he was wound up as tight as a watch spring. He had a great sense of humor, and there was many a difficult time when we both were able to laugh our way out of a situation that could have plunged us into gloom. As I write these lines I don't know if George is still alive, but if he is and he happens to read this book, I want him to know that I owe him a great debt.

The third task to which I assigned myself was to "run" my agents in a manner that not only kept them safe, but that maximized their usefulness. In other words, could existing agents do more and better things for us? Enter the entire subject of "agent handling." Some operations officers are brilliant agent handlers: they motivate and communicate a sense of enthusiasm to their agents. Other officers are not as talented, and a given agent operation can quickly become a fairly pedestrian matter because full use is not being made of the agent's potential. There has to be good chemistry between an agent and his case officer, and if there isn't the entire operation will suffer. Unfortunately, all too many case officers fail to both motivate and understand their agents. As one might suspect, the case officer – agent relationship is absolutely crucial. After all, the agent is putting his life in the case officer's hands, is usually frightened to death, and very often can be a very peculiar bird indeed. I never had an agent who did not require some special treatment in order to keep him "happy" and productive. This is where the case officer's personality and people skills play a tremendously important role. A dull and unimaginative officer who is unresponsive to the unique mental makeup and psychological needs of a given agent is bound to place a case in trouble. In my career I repeatedly saw instances, for example, where a rather plodding agent has been turned into a producer of significant intelligence simply because his case officer understood the right buttons to push.

Yes, the case officer business involves the manipulation of human beings: in fact it is fundamental to the job. "Manipulating" people has a negative connotation – yet all of us are busy manipulating people no matter what we are doing in our lives. As a practical matter, everyone is busy manipulating everyone else, and it is ludicrous to deny that this is a fundamental aspect of the human condition. In the case officer world, manipulating an agent boils down to making the agent productive and keeping him safe.

The most egregious examples of poor case officer handling of an agent usually come when a newly recruited source is "turned over" to a successor case officer. Almost by definition the recruiting officer has had a very special relationship with the agent: the relationship which resulted in the agent's agreement to enter into a clandestine relationship.

This is not easy for most agents, and it is frequently – perhaps always – the case that the new agent has come to have an enormous reliance on the recruiting officer. A bond has been forged, and the test of a real recruitment comes in the willingness of the agent to accept a "turnover" to a new case officer. An agent who has been truly recruited will accept the turnover, but it is up to the new case officer to reinforce the agent's commitment to the relationship. The new case officer has to quickly accomplish several important tasks, the first of which is to reassure the agent that his safety is paramount in the officer's mind. The second key task is to establish positive rapport with the agent. I have personally seen agents who were recruited after long and hard development be "turned off" by a successor case officer. It is up to managers to ensure that there is a match between the case officer and the agent, but sometimes it is not possible to make a perfect "pair" between the two. In that instance one hopes that the new case officer can rise to the occasion, since if he does not the agent may well decide to terminate the relationship.

This is as good a time as any to discuss the subject of agent termination, which has given rise to the phrase "terminate with extreme prejudice" in movies and novels. Trust me, I never once heard that term used in all my years of dealing with agents. There are several reasons why agents are terminated, the most obvious of which is that the agent decides that he doesn't want to continue the relationship. If an agent makes such a decision, and he is a valuable source, his "handlers" have to try mightily to keep his services. But if the agent will have none of it, that is the end of the relationship. The "separation" is amicable. In other instances we decide that we no longer want to make use of a given agent and it is decided to terminate him. What this actually means is that an amicable understanding is reached between the agent and the case officer: there are no threats or "punishments" involved. Obviously in either instance it is in the agent's best interest to keep the fact of his relationship secret, and to our benefit to do the same thing. I have terminated agents for nonproduction; because they had no access to intelligence of value; or because they simply could not be trained to operate safely and the risks involved in the operation far outweighed any possible value that the agent had to us.

Again I stress that these terminations are amicable. We certainly do not attempt to blackmail an agent into continuing contact with us if it is his choice to sever the relationship. Blackmail simply does not work and, essentially, is unethical.

One time that terminations can be a bit dicey is when we have determined that the agent is a "double" – meaning that he is working for another intelligence service. We generally do not want to tip our hand by revealing that we are aware of the agent's double role, so we might have to do some imaginative explaining as to why we no longer want to be in contact with the man. Inasmuch as we often have to conceal our knowledge that the man is working for another service, this can take some real and inventive skill.

Another reason to terminate an agent is because he is a fabricator: he invents intelligence information, either deliberately to mislead us (which generally means he is being controlled by a hostile service) or simply as a means of making a living. Again the task for the case officer is to withdraw smoothly from the operation.

Finally, I wanted to recruit some real agents. As I have noted before, this in many ways is the acid test of a really fine case officer. I found this to be both exciting and challenging, and I was fortunate to have had some success.

A couple of stories on myself:

I was meeting an agent, an intelligence officer from an East European communist nation who was seen on a very irregular basis whenever he was able to leave his country. He happened to turn and, after giving the appropriate signals indicating that he wanted a meeting, I had the task of picking him up in a car in the dark of night to receive information from him and to pass him additional requirements. It was in the middle of the hottest season, with 100% relative humidity and temperature approaching 100°F. As a precaution I met the agent while using a disguise; in this case wearing a bushy black mustache with my blonde hair dyed black. The meeting went well except that the air conditioner in the car failed, and both of us were pouring sweat. After a time I noticed that he was looking at me rather strangely, and when I reached up to wipe my forehead I discovered why: because of the heat and humidity the black hair dye was running down my face. Exactly as I discovered this my mustache fell off, and I succeeded in catching it in midair before it hit my lap. This is definitely not covered in the agent training manuals, and the situation was so ridiculous that I burst out laughing. So, to his credit, did the intelligence officer/agent. We both laughed uproariously for some minutes. When I dropped him off he made the sage comment: "life in intelligence business does have its lighter moments, doesn't it."

In another instance, when I was also meeting an intelligence officer from Eastern Europe, the meeting was arranged to take place at a "safe house" - an apartment in a five-story building. This was a crucial meeting, as the agent had to be debriefed; passed new communications plans and collection requirements; and be given a fairly large amount of money. The meeting was scheduled to take place at 2 o'clock in the morning, when the streets would be deserted, and I could easily detect any surveillance that might be placed on me. Just as I was about to round a corner and enter the building, a taxicab roared up behind me, turned the corner, and slammed to a stop not 10 feet in front of me. I froze, trying my unsuccessful best to look like a telephone pole. The driver and the occupant of the front passenger seat jumped out of the taxicab, ran around to the back of the vehicle, opened the trunk, and removed a large and obviously heavy package. They unceremoniously dumped the package on the street at my feet and sped off in the cab.

Concerned that an event like this would take place in the middle of the night when there were no other vehicles on the streets, I peered down at the package, which turned out to be a human body poorly wrapped in an old piece of fabric. My first thought was that my agent had been compromised and was being delivered to me – dead. I moved some of the fabric aside and saw a male face that could not possibly be my agent.

I carried on with the meeting.

To this day I have no idea what the whole scene was about... except that someone obviously wanted to get rid of a body.

The highlight of this tour came just as I was beginning to question whether a career in the Agency was all that I thought it should be. There was no question that what I had been doing was challenging and required my hundred percent commitment and effort, but, in taking the long view, it seemed to me that I was not, in fact, contributing significantly to the interests of the United States. In brief, and this is not an uncommon concern amongst junior officers, while you worked your heart out the "product" did not seem to make much difference in the great scheme of things. As I was nearing the end of my tour I thought it was a good time to review what I thought about the intelligence business after two years of training and two years of field service. So I quite intentionally stood back a bit in an effort to decide whether I would or would not continue in the Service.

My "review" was complicated by the fact that Bob Andrews, the old and dear friend from my university days who had persuaded me to take a shot at law school at the University of Arizona, contacted me with an extraordinary offer. By this time Bob had established his law practice, a very successful one, in California. Bob's offer, which came right out of the blue, was to fund my going to three years of law school – paying both my tuition and providing a stipend that would support me and my family. Bob's only condition was that I join him in his practice once I had completed law school. He urged me to apply for entry to the University of Southern California College of Law: if I was accepted, Bob's offer would see me through law school without financial burden. I made the application and was accepted. So there I was with one of those life-changing decisions: remain in the service for a career, or go on to law school and become a lawyer. My brief exposure to law school suggested to me that I didn't want to become a lawyer. I knew, however, that I had the skills to successfully negotiate law school, and I believed – as Bob insisted – that I could be a very good lawyer. Perhaps, thought I, while law school was a pain, <u>practicing</u> law, particularly being involved in litigation, could be a challenge and a very satisfying career. All of this took place in a two or three month period, and I must admit the offer was an interesting one.

It was also, of course, a deeply disturbing conundrum, particularly given what I regarded as my lifelong commitment to government service.

I had not made up my mind over which course to take when I had one of those career breakthroughs that once and for all persuaded me that I had chosen the right profession. One of my agents, an East

European military officer with whom I had been working hard for months, was able to obtain the plans for the use of a Soviet surface-to-air missile system which was deployed in North Vietnam and which was killing a number of our aircraft and pilots. This was the height of the Vietnam War, and of "Rolling Thunder" – our massive air offensive against North Vietnam. It was alleged that the air defense system that the Soviets had built up to defend Hanoi was the most extensive in history, and it certainly was taking its toll on American pilots and aircraft.

To have the information on how this missile system worked should, we thought, help defeat it. We forwarded the information to Washington and were later told that indeed the information did result in greatly reduced aircraft losses, at least for a significant period.

Any doubts I had as to whether a career in the Service could have a positive effect on our national security vanished. I profusely thanked Bob for his extraordinary and generous offer, and determined to dig in for the long haul.

I suspect this wavering is not uncommon amongst junior officers, and it certainly paid dividends for me in that it allowed me to pause for a moment and to consider whether I had made the right career choice. Thanking Bob, I never looked back.

One of the compensations for living in one of the world's most wretched cities was that we were able to travel into northeastern India, to the state Assam, where there were some fabulous game parks at the foothills of the Himalayas. One of the most fascinating of such journeys was a two-week "tiger hunt" in the border area just south of the Himalayan kingdom of Bhutan. I want to quickly point out that I didn't have the slightest interest in actually killing a tiger, but I did want to hunt one to see if I could actually get one of the big cats in my rifle sights: the chase was everything.

Through the courtesy of a friend I wound up in a hunting camp which consisted of three or four huts built high on stilts to keep wild animals out. The camp was deep in a forest reserve where tiger hunting had not yet been banned, and was surrounded by barbed wire – again to keep predatory animals like tigers and leopards out. In keeping with local customs, I brought a servant along, which caused quite a sensation among the locals, as my "man" Apa Rao, in his white uniform and brass buttons, took over the management of the entire camp and in general presided over everything and everyone. There were probably 20 or 30 local natives in the camp, which included six elephants, their keepers, and various hangers-on whose job it was to feed and water the elephants, keep the camp cleaned up, and in general do all manner tasks that revolved around the hunt. I was the first white man that many of the locals had ever seen, and they persisted in calling me the "English Sahib," which roughly translates into "Mr. Englishman." In a way it was all a vaguely surreal event.

Picture being awakened before dawn by the noble Apa Rao, who handed me a cup of scalding hot coffee. Rao had laid out my clothing for the day, cleaned my muddy jungle boots, and made us all breakfast. At night the situation was reversed, as Rao was waiting when we got back to the camp at sundown. I removed my sweaty clothing and stood buck naked next to a fire while Rao poured hot water over me while I soaped up and rinsed off. Then I stepped into the next set of clean clothing that Rao had prepared for me.

We hunted from elephant back: every morning at dawn three elephants turned up, and my three-person hunting party climbed up on their backs and went forth into the jungle. To spend two weeks closely associated with an elephant, rifle in my hands, sitting immediately behind the elephant "driver," was an experience right out of 19th century India. Every minute was sheer delight. While searching for tiger we also hunted "for the pot," which, in this case, meant the huge wild boar that were common in the area, but which were so dangerous that the natives could not use them as a source of food. On my first day of hunting, I was very fortunate in that, coming into a large clearing, we saw a boar about 100 yards away. Since I was "first gun" it was my shot, and I dropped the boar. I say fortunate because this proved to my hosts I could actually shoot – something they were a little apprehensive about. The boar fed the entire camp for days.

There were tigers all around the camp: it was mating season, and we could hear them calling to each other as we sat around the fire for the evening's several glasses of Scotch whiskey. We knew they were there, but I only saw a tiger on one occasion, and that after days of scouring the jungle. I had my sights on him for approximately one second, and quietly said "bang, I gotcha." Again, the hunt was the thing.

I came to have great respect and affection for the elephant that had been assigned to me. I am convinced that elephants are approximately as smart as humans, and that every elephant has its own personality. I was a little shaken when first introduced to "my" elephant, as I was told that he had killed his previous "driver." This seemed to me to suggest that the elephant might just like killing human beings. I was reassured, however, when told the rest of the story: it seems the departed "driver" (the Hindustani term is "Mahoot") had stolen the elephant's sugar rations. Since sugarcane is the key to winning an elephant's heart, and this theft went on for some time, I was informed that the elephants' killing the man was fully justified. I took great care to each day personally feed the elephant a substantial quantity of sugarcane... about double his normal ration.

At the end of my first assignment I was transferred to the capital city (or another city in the country), which was a step up because it was swarming with potential targets: aside from a huge Soviet presence, all of the Communist East European countries had extensive representation. It was, as the military says, a "target rich" environment.

So my family and I made the trek to the new post, where I served for the next three years. In many ways, it was more of the same, with the added excitement that war between India and Pakistan erupted in the sub-continent; a war which also saw the bloody creation of the new state of Bangladesh. With the area in turmoil, anti-American sentiment ran high, which resulted in some amusing incidents. One of which was that the Canadian Embassy, anxious not to be associated with America, painted Canadian flags on all their diplomatic vehicles. This was a gross violation of diplomatic protocol, which we found tremendously amusing. The British and Australians did no such thing. But, as I had discovered, official Canadians overseas often have a serious identity problem since most foreigners take English-speaking Canadians to be Americans. Our view was that the Canadians were being typically chicken, and that their behavior represented a massive inferiority complex. I remember talking to a Canadian Embassy officer who was bitterly complaining about being taken for an American: I advised him that what he and his colleagues should do was to wear fur parkas and go about speaking in Eskimo. He was not amused.

My decision to remain in the Service, proved to have been the correct one. By the time I left with five years of field service under my belt, I felt that I had certainly achieved "journeyman" case officer status. I had demonstrated that I could run agents well, and I was able to make a few high level recruitments in the extensive Communist Block community.

A few comments on my personal and family life during these years: Superficially, living appeared to be easy – housing was good, servants were plentiful, and the social whirl was endless – and for many foreigners life was indeed very pleasant. For those of us in the intelligence business, however, things were not nearly as comfortable. There was first the inevitable toll that was taken by the fact that one's spouse did not have a clue what one was involved in, and yet for many days and nights operations officers were away at occasionally lunatic hours and with remarkable frequency. One's wife (and in my day all case officers were male) had to be very trusting indeed, and frequently had to fill the gaps occasioned by an absent husband. To say that our wives were important, not only to our personal but also to our professional lives, is a wild understatement. It was not just that the press of case officer business impinged on family life, but the health and welfare of our children was of some concern. In the matter of health, the place could be a deathtrap, particularly for people coming out of the relatively sterile and benign health environments of Europe and America. One had to be extremely careful what and where one ate, and where one's children ate. For a wife, keeping a kitchen free of all the local weird diseases and maladies was a full-time job. Yes, there was a cook and perhaps a cook's helper, but a wife had to fight a never ending battle to maintain the requisite standards of care in food preparation. Water had to be boiled for 20 minutes before it could be considered safe to drink. Leafy vegetables were out of the question as they would soak up water from contaminated soil. All vegetables had to be soaked in a solution of Clorox and water before they could be eaten. It was relatively easy to keep one's home safe, but when one ate out (unless it was in another household operating under the same rules) one had to be very careful.

Virtually all of us had an active or latent case of dysentery from having to eat outside our homes. Cholera and malaria were rampant, and there were still risks of exotic diseases like Blackwater Fever. From a health perspective this was definitely not the suburban USA.

There was one particularly frightening experience involving my four-year-old son, Guy. He had gone to a birthday party of some friends and, escaping his nanny, had been given and eaten an ice cream cone. He promptly came down with some sort of dysentery that caused his fever to spike at 104°. We called our family doctor, a personal friend, who said he would get to the house in 45 minutes. In the meantime we were to put Guy in a bathtub full of cool water and add as much ice as we could to the water – this to break his fever. Into the tub went Guy along with a large number of ice cubes. He began shivering, and plaintively asked "Daddy, why are you doing this to me." It was heartrending. It was one of two times that I was badly shaken by placing my family in jeopardy simply because of my job. I had to argue with my conscience: it was all very well for me to take a job in a place where sickness was a constant concern, but I felt that I had no right to place my family at grave risk. Fortunately, Susan was always solid as a rock as various near-calamities befell us, told me to stop fretting and that we would, of course, carry on. The picture of that little boy shivering in a bathtub full of ice water is with me to this day. I am terribly proud of how both my children and my wife put up with the stresses, physical and mental, that frequently came with our overseas assignments. Without them I could not possibly have continued.

We had excellent schools for my two young sons, but I found it impossible to spend as much time with them as I wanted. Not only was there the press of business, frequently a nighttime activity on top of a full day at work, but there was a very necessary social aspect to the job. Many nights there would be two or perhaps three invitations to cocktail and dinner parties: many of which simply had to be accepted. I tried my best to see as much as possible of my family, but there was always the nagging fact that I had to be away from them far more often than would have been the case if we were living at home in the States.

It was necessary to get some relief from the pressures of the job. We did this by making frequent visits to magnificent game parks.

My favorite spot was in the middle of the Jim Corbett National Park, named for a British-era Forest Officer who had gained fame as the killer of various dangerous man-eating tigers. We stayed at a small "forest rest house" in the middle of the park. The place had been built early in the 20th century for the use of British Indian Forest Service officers, had running water and sparse but adequate furniture. Surrounded by the usual barbed wire, the house was located near the bank of a river which runs through the park. Indian crocodiles, some well over 10 feet long, inhabited the river and lazed in the sun on the riverbank immediately below the house. Using the house as a base of operations we rode around the park by car and on elephant-back looking at the wild game. There were also several observation towers overlooking waterholes and salt licks, and it was great fun to go up in the tower at dawn and dusk when the animals would come out to drink. The boys loved to be in the parks, and we saw all manner of wildlife – from exotic birds to tiger, leopard, many species of deer, and lots of crocodile. I had shifted from hunting with a rifle to photography, and it was just a rewarding to try to get photos of the elusive big game.

I found that a few days with my family at one of these game parks was excellent R&R: rest and recreation. It was a tremendous way to step away from the stress and strain of the job. In fact, rather than take advantage of free travel to the normal "R&R points" like Singapore, we preferred to go into the Indian bush and jungle. Our theory was that anyone could visit Singapore, but very few people could be transplanted into magnificent Indian wildlife preserves. These trips were doubly wonderful since it was time alone with my family: we were absolutely cut off from the rest of the world – no telephones, no electric lights, and no obligations other than to take advantage of the forest primeval. Many of the happiest days of this time of my life were spent in these game parks.

To give an example of just how close to nature we were, one pleasant afternoon I took my son Colin for short walk down to look at the crocodiles. Just as we exited the barbed wire which surrounded the house, a mature leopard stood up in the waist-high grass not 5 feet from where we were standing. It was hard to tell whether we or the leopard were more surprised by this impromptu meeting, and for a split second I had the horrifying thought that I was exposing my son to "death by leopard." Fortunately, the animal had better things to do than hang around humans and he bolted away.

5

THE PERSIAN GULF

My family and I returned to the U.S. from the Indian sub-continent after our five-year stint in the early summer of 1973 - I assumed for a two-year tour at Headquarters. Rotation between field and Headquarters is a constant one for all NCS officers. With few exceptions this is a good system, since officers overseas need to learn how to wage the bureaucratic wars both within Headquarters and between Headquarters and the rest of the foreign affairs community. Traditionally, the most important job of Headquarters officers is to support the field, and there are "Branches" in each of the "Area Divisions" of the NCS whose job it is to support specific Stations. In a way, each Branch represents a Station's interest at Headquarters, and it is fairly common for an officer returning from a given foreign posting to be assigned to the "country branch", thus giving the Headquarters branch the benefit of his or her knowledge of a given Station. It works the other way as well, and a Headquarters officer slated for a specific assignment overseas is usually attached to its corresponding branch at Headquarters "to read in" for at least a few months before going out to the field. The system has great advantages for officers going in both directions.

I was fortunate to be assigned to a Branch, where I worked for Clair George, a brilliant operations officer for whom I had worked when we were both overseas. Clair would later go on to become first the Associate Deputy Director for Operations, and eventually the Deputy Director for Operations - as such he was head of the National Clandestine Service. Clair, whose expertise in the world of clandestine operations was matched only by his acerbic humor, was a mentor of mine at Headquarters, just as he had been in the field. I could not have been more fortunate in having Clair as a role model, and the Service as a whole benefited greatly from his sure hand at the wheel.

Sadly, Clair was badly tarnished – without justification – when the Iran-Contra affair made the headlines many years later. I never met a man with a more certain grasp of what the spy business was all about, or who attached such importance to probity and operating within the law. I do not intend to go into the details of the Iran-Contra business, something that would probably take several books to cover, but I do know that Clair had no part in any illegal activities related to the matter. Along with several other Agency officers, he was made a sacrificial goat. Worse was to come, as after Clair retired from the service he first lost Mary, his much-loved wife of many years, and was then afflicted with macular degeneration – in his last years he was blind. I know that I speak for a number of senior NCS officers when I say that Clair was a man of unimpeachable integrity, skill and great good humor: we shall not soon see his likes again.

After something less than a year at my Headquarters assignment, I was, to my great surprise, chosen to become Chief of Station (COS) in one of the small gulf kingdoms. I barely knew where it was, and when I said so was rather abruptly informed that it was in the Persian Gulf and thus was an important place to be. The fact was that for many years we had looked to others to keep an eye on matters in the Gulf. That had ended, and there was now a "hole" that had to be plugged.

As I was just 33 years old I was thrilled with the assignment. I had no delusions in thinking that my new Station was going to be the center of the universe, as it was a very small Station in a very large pond. At any rate, I had to do some frantic reading to catch up with affairs in the Persian Gulf.

I was delighted to find out that my new posting was a very westernized little country and that the language of the country was basically English, which was a blessing since I spoke no Arabic.

I arrived alone along with a brand-new Ambassador, who turned out to be not only a superlative Foreign Service Officer, but a great friend. Basically the only thing wrong with the assignment was the weather: two or three months of winter are gorgeous, after which the heat and humidity are absolutely dreadful.

This assignment provided me with my first practical exposure to the differences between Sunni and Shia Islam, and to the extent of the hostility between these two major denominations of Islam. The theological complexity of the schism between these two bodies of Muslim thought is fairly mind-boggling, and quite beyond the scope of this book: what is important is that the vast majority of the Islamic world — perhaps 90% — is Sunni. The simplest way to define the two groups is that Sunnis regard Abu Bakr as the first caliph (leader) of the faith, while Shia Muslims consider the Prophet Mohammed's son-in-law Ali to be the first caliph. Endless animosity and conflict between the two denominations has gone on since the death of the Prophet. Of all Muslim countries, only Iran and Iraq have majority Shia populations, and of these two countries only Iraq has a significant minority of Sunnis.

While we would later fight two major wars against Saddam Hussein's Iraq, at the time the threat posed by Saddam was largely represented by his attempt to establish a government he would control in my small fiefdom. Such a development was greatly feared up and down the Gulf, and by the United States because a government dominated by Saddam would adversely threaten American security interests in the oil-rich Gulf.

But for the weather, life was very pleasant. We had a very nice house and I even bought a sailboat, although sailing in the warm waters of the Gulf heat was a challenge. In fact, except for those few winter months, it was ghastly. I settled in happily with my small Station, kept busy at my work, and in general thoroughly enjoyed the experience.

I expected to do a normal tour, but my masters at Headquarters had other ideas. Just short of two years into my tour I received a visit from Dewey Claridge, then a senior officer in my Area Division, with the news that Headquarters wanted me to transfer to Tehran, Iran — immediately.

I did not take this news well. I had never served in Iran or even visited the place, but all I had ever heard while in the Gulf was that Iranians were horrible people and that it was a terrible country to live in. At the time, the Shah was still in power, and it seemed that Iran was something of a sleeping giant. My question back to Dewey was "what had I done wrong to deserve this punishment?" Had I no friends at Headquarters? I carefully explained that I thought my Station was doing what it should be doing; had a lot more to do; and that I wanted to do it. Besides, said I, I don't speak Farsi and had never heard a good word about the country or serving there. Further, I understood that it was a very large Station mostly involved in liaison activities with the Shah's government. That did not sound like a place I would like to serve.

Dewey heard me out and then explained that this was a "directed assignment." In other words, Headquarters was giving me no choice. Dewey patiently explained that I would be the number three guy in the Station (the COS was a very senior and much older officer); that I would have no liaison responsibilities, and that I was "needed" there. There was, he said, a requirement for "new blood and new direction" in the Station. Besides, said Dewey, there was a promotion involved.

I am amused to be reminded of Dewey's visit daily: I have a small set of miniature British Indian Army soldiers on a shelf in my library – a gift from Dewey on this visit. Dewey had somehow heard of my interest and long study of the British Indian Army, and had thoughtfully brought along the small set of soldiers.

While not in the least pleased with this turn of events, I nevertheless felt I had no choice but to agree to accept the assignment. Claridge quite rightly said that not having the language was no bar to serving in Iran: "anyone worth talking to speaks English" was the way that Dewey put it. So I went home and told my wife and children the bad news. As always, my happy campers put the best face on it, and we all agreed that we would go to Tehran and make the best of it.

This brings up the question of "directed assignments:" this was the first of three such events in my career, each of which marked a major change in what I had thought I would be doing. In my view I pretty much had to go along with whatever my superiors wanted me to do, the only exception being if an assignment were to have serious adverse effect on my family. On two other occasions carefully made plans for new assignments were abruptly canceled by directives from on high - in the succeeding two instances by orders from the Director of CIA. It is understood that the "needs of the Service" control an individual officer's assignments, and that is generally a very good rule. Obviously the NCS cannot force an individual to accept an assignment if it is patently clear that the individual is absolutely opposed to it. There is no point in having thoroughly unhappy officers in any assignment. My view always was that if one received an unexpected and not particularly attractive assignment, one should take it with good humor and spirit. Which I always did, and, interestingly enough in retrospect, I was always glad that I had.

At a farewell party that someone gave for us one of our Arab friends came up to me, clutched my arms, looked me straight in the eye and said: "you do not deserve this" – meaning the assignment to Tehran. I couldn't have agreed more.

6

IRAN

Little did I realize when I arrived in Iran in the spring of 1976 just how much impact the assignment was going to have on me and my family; and just how important "the Iran problem" was going to become for the United States and the world in the following years … in fact, until today.

The Iran I arrived in struck me as a vast Potemkin village: an edifice dominated by the Shah and his secret police and built on sand. Aside from Tehran's insane traffic, living in the city was pleasant enough. Tehran came complete with a large US military presence, a PX, a large American School, and even a U.S. military-run radio station that played American hit songs. I quickly learned that all Iranians believed in – or, more correctly, paid lip service to – the Shah. It was a servile society, held in check by the belief that Savak, the Shah's internal security service, was everywhere and knew everything. There was absolutely no such thing as free political expression, and Savak saw to it that the society almost literally worshiped the Shah and his government. It was definitely an Alice in Wonderland environment.

Outwardly, Iran appeared to be stable, and certainly as of the time I arrived and for at least a year thereafter, any radical change in the country was deemed absolutely impossible. Little things made an impression on me: no Iranian would refer to the Shah by that title alone – it was always "His Imperial Majesty." I was hugely amused by one of the Shah's titles: "The Shadow of God on Earth," which even for famously unctuous Iranians was a little taxing. There was a universal conviction that CIA manipulated the Shah, and that the United States was behind every move he made: and certainly behind his autocratic and despotic rule. Iranians are great believers in conspiracies: behind every event lurks some conspiracy. This tendency colors their view of the world and of themselves.

In fact, in the 1950's CIA did manipulate political activities in the country in order to keep it from falling into the hands of the Soviet Union's Iranian puppets, and thus probably saved the Shah from being overthrown. This fact was well known to every Iranian who had the slightest interest in Iran's history. The truth was, however, that the Shah had long since sailed out from under US influence. He had brought about the great rise in petroleum prices in the early 1970s, single-handedly throwing the world briefly into economic chaos. I learned that the US government literally could bring very little or no pressure to bear on "The Shadow of God."

The Shah was, however, a staunch military ally, and the United States was selling vast quantities of military hardware to Iran, hence the large US military and US military contractor presence.

Many in Congress objected to this military relationship, citing the fact that it was a very visible expression of American support for a "tin pot dictator." The principal reason for our support for the Shah's government in the military arena was as a counterweight: first to Iraq under Saddam Hussein; and second to the Soviet Union, with which Iran has a common border.

At first, Iran struck me as something of a lotus land, with its entire government and educated population munching happily on lotus leaves. The real perception of the Shah by the lower elements of society was unknown, but was assumed to be the devotion the Shah called for from his people. How terribly wrong this assumption was soon became clear.

Iran, alone in a Sunni Muslim world, has a majority Shia population. The Shah himself paid no attention to religion at all and, in fact, in many ways suppressed the Shia clergy in the country. All mosques were under Savak surveillance, and woe be unto the Shia clergyman who deviated from a worshipful respect for the Shah and his government.

I must digress: half a century ago it was frequently asserted that Islam (the name of the religion, the practitioners of which are called

Muslims) has no clergy. This is certainly true if you compare Islam to the well-structured Roman Catholic or Protestant faiths of the West. The fact of the matter is, however, that there has long been a tradition of Islamic clerics: students of the Holy Quran, who achieved considerable power in their religious schools and in the mosques. In the mid-1970s it was assumed that Muslim clerics had no power, neither in Iran nor in the other dictatorships in the Middle East. Since then the world has become aware of the enormous power these clerics now wield. Iranian clergy ran the revolution that overthrew the Shah, and now run Iran. In much of the rest of the Middle East, Muslim clerics are now contesting for power in the wake of the fall of the various dictatorships that were overthrown in the so-called "Arab Spring."

The Muslim clergy goes through long and arduous training, all of which is focused on the Quran and various interpretations of it. This means that their knowledge is an inch wide and a mile deep, and their worldview reflects this upbringing. It is not an exaggeration to say that Muslim clerics, after their many years of intensive study of the Quran – and only the Quran – look at the world through Quran–colored lenses. These are men, and only men, who by training and thinking are about as far from any sort of "secular" or "contemporary world" viewpoint as is possible. In many ways they are true 10th century men.

Islam has laid a dead hand on progress and development, certainly in the Middle Eastern world. Ultraconservative Muslim clergy have for centuries dominated religious thought and action in the Middle East. This was even true under the Ottoman Empire, which, while it was the dominant power in the Western world in the 15th and 16th centuries, had atrophied into a repressive and economically and technologically backward state by the 19th century. The reason for this was that the clergy advising the various Sultans rejected virtually all of the intellectual flowering of the West – and it's technological advances as well. The story is famously told of an Ottoman Emperor who in the 19th century wanted to send a team to Europe to study the development of railroads, the telegraph, transport systems, etc. The Emperor's spiritual advisors told him that this would be impossible, as the Quran forbade the introduction of "infidel thinking." The Emperor did not send his team.

Much is made of the fact that the word Islam translates to "submission." And that the Quran can and should be interpreted as the testament of a religion of peace and progress. There is as much truth to that statement as there would be to defining Christianity in the same way. As Western history shows, just as Europe was divided by religious wars for centuries, with opposing sides claiming justification and the legitimacy of warfare from passages in the Bible, the same is true of the Quran. This is a roundabout way of saying that both Christianity and Islam can use their respective holy books to justify war and aggression against "non-believers." In the Western world, religious wars are out of fashion. In the Islamic world, religious wars are increasingly the "in" thing.

In much of the Middle Eastern Islamic world the Quran is interpreted as legitimizing <u>any</u> acts of violence against "non-believers" in the faith. For those who choose to accept this interpretation of the Quran, there is no act too violent in pursuing Islam's absolute mandate to convert all of humanity to its precepts.

Islam expanded from its very beginnings by the sword, and every Islamic nation in the world got that way because of Islam's early "convert or die" philosophy, which began with newly converted Bedouin tribesmen riding out of the Saudi desert to conquer and convert the world. Like Christianity, Islam can be a religion of peace, and in some places in the world it continues to be this. In the Middle East, however, Islam is now becoming a religion of war against the non-believer: once more recourse is being had to the sword. It is interesting to note that not only Christians are considered an abomination deserving of death or conversion: Islam is very evenhanded, and every faith in the world but Islam is an enemy.

The interesting complication to this interpretation of the Quran is the division between Sunni Islam and Shia Islam. Each side in this schism believes the other guilty of apostasy; for a Shia, in fact, the Sunni is even a greater villain than a Christian – and vice versa. For various reasons Shia Islam, represented largely by Iran, has been the more contentious of the two sides of the faith.

Islam is not just a religious faith as we in the West consider religion. It is an entire system of social and governmental control and regimentation, and every facet of an individual's life is controlled by some specific rule or other. If one chooses to interpret the Quran as does the ruling religious clique in Iran, the precepts of the faith govern all social, legal, personal and governmental aspects of society. It is absolutely impossible for a strictly conservative and radical Muslim to accept the fundamentals of the American Declaration of Independence or of our Constitution's Bill of Rights: both of which stand in direct contradiction to the precepts of the "one true faith."

BACK TO IRAN, CIRCA 1977

The Shah was fully aware of the latent power of the clergy in Iran, and for that reason he had seen fit to exile the most vocal of his clerical critics. Several ayatollahs - a term of religious distinction, applied to clerical elders who are particularly deeply steeped in the Quran – were in exile in Iraq, which was dominated by Saddam Hussein. The "greatest" Ayatollah of all was living in France: the Ayatollah Khomeini. These outspoken clergymen based their criticism of the Shah on his obviously steering Iran into a secular world a la Europe or the United States: clearly abandoning the precepts of Islam. Of course this is exactly what the Shah was attempting to do. This not only offended the religious sensibilities of the senior clerics, but it also denied them the power in society that they felt was due to them. In other words many ayatollahs criticized the Shah on both religious grounds and for very practical political purposes - he denied them the power which they believed was theirs by right. By placing his most senior clerical enemies in exile, and by Savak having its thumb on the low-ranked clergy in every mosque across the land, the Shah felt he had the lid nicely on the pot.

What he did not realize was the level of discontent stirring amongst ordinary Iranians, discontent which, once ignited, swept down on him and destroyed his regime in a matter of months.

There was, in fact, a nascent opposition to the Shah, largely centered on the Ayatollah Khomeini in France. A handful of Western educated Iranians around Khomeini ostensibly led what they viewed as a reform movement: for most of these non-clerical activists that meant creating a constitutional monarchy which would limit the Shah's authority. I discovered that neither the Station nor the Embassy's Foreign Service Officers had any contacts with, or lines into, this small group of nonreligious "anti-Shah" people. There was certainly no contact with or information about the anti-Shah clergy. Both Station and Embassy operated on the basis that the Shah's authority was unchallenged and unchallengeable. I was not surprised that the Embassy had no contacts with this amorphous "opposition." The State Department's position was that the Shah was an ally who was firmly in power, and that any contact with persons – clergy or otherwise – who were opposed to the Shah was unnecessary, and would be immediately detected by Savak. That would lead to reprimands from the Shah and risk our "good" relations with him. There was some truth to this, as there is no doubt that if Embassy officers were openly in contact with Iranian "dissidents" such contacts would quickly come to the Shah's attention, and risk his ire.

That the Station had no such contacts *did* surprise me, since it is traditionally CIA's job to have covert contacts with opposition forces in any country. There were none. The Station, too, was busily munching on lotus leaves. It became clear to me that I had been sent to Tehran because Headquarters was unhappy with the Station's lack of sources of any kind: either in the Iranian "establishment" or amongst any latent anti-Shah groups. This is not to say that Headquarters was concerned that the Shah's grip on power might be challenged – that idea had crossed no one's mind, and in general Headquarters, like the State Department, thought that the Shah faced no serious threat from any opposition groups. My job, leading a small group of case officers in the Station, was to develop and recruit clandestine reporting sources to fill the enormous holes in our knowledge of political developments in Iran.

These things take time: one does not simply say "let's go out and recruit agents who report on what might really be happening," particularly when the "target" was ill-defined. Generally speaking, we did not know who the secular Iranians who gravitated around the Ayatollah Khomeini were, or what they wanted. We essentially knew nothing.

We did, however, know that having direct contact with senior Muslim clergymen was out of the question – it was clear that the entire clergy believed that the United States was the devil incarnate; that it would be absolutely impossible to gain access to them; and that they would reject any attempts at contact out of hand.

While castigating the Station for its lack of sources of a political nature, I must make clear that there was a reason for this: what we call "liaison equities." We were cooperating with the Shah, through Savak, in maintaining several very high-tech "listening posts" targeting the Soviet Union. From mountaintops in northernmost Iran the electronic "view" into Soviet missile test ranges was very clear. We had for years, with the cooperation of the Iranians, maintained these installations, which provided critical information on the Soviet ballistic missile programs. The importance of these sites was great, and for some years their continuation and maintenance was the Station's key mission: they were gathering strategic information of vital interest to the United States. Given their importance, "fooling around with a pack of crazy mullahs and their few known secular allies" was considered inadvisable.

There is no question but that the electronic collection sites represented an enormous investment of money and people, and that they were the most important activity that the Station was engaged in. In my view, however, that should be no bar to quiet, very professional work to recruit human sources to keep us apprised of future political developments in the country. If for no other reason than that the Shah was actually a human being who would someday die, and that it would be in our interest to know that the turnover of power to his Crown Prince son would be smooth.

In sum, while Iran appeared to be stable, and the Shah's rule unchallenged, we knew that the senior clergy was bitterly opposed to him. What we did not know was whether there was a serious anti-Shah current in the country.

Starting in 1977 there were increasing reports - by word-of-mouth, since the press, radio and newspapers were all controlled by the Shah - of demonstrations in some of the major cities south of Tehran. These demonstrations grew in size and frequency, and soon shifted to include Tehran. It was initially unclear as to what was sparking the demonstrations, and indeed what their goal was. It fairly soon became obvious that the demonstrations were not spontaneous, but were in some manner being controlled by persons unknown.

One must remember that every village, every town, and every area of every city in Iran has a mosque. The faithful are called to prayer five times a day, with major religious "services" taking place on Fridays. This constitutes a powerful built-in network to mobilize people - a network that almost magically began to oppose the Shah.

Demonstrations were at first met by the police, without success, although considerable force was used against the demonstrators. As they grew in size and frequency we began to take notice. The common theme evinced by demands from the demonstrators was essentially a call to "return to Islam." This was a code phrase which meant "get rid of the Shah." The Shah took note, and in an attempt to mollify the clergy – which was obviously leading the demonstrations – he allowed the Ayatollah Khomeini to return to the country. This was probably a miscalculation, since when the Ayatollah landed at Tehran's airport he was greeted by hundreds of thousands of delirious supporters: Iranians saw this as a clear indication that the Shah's grip was loosening.

More and bigger demonstrations became the norm – demonstrations that were often brilliantly led by women wearing the *chador* ... the traditional black full body garment. The Shah called out the Army to halt the demonstrations. This failed, as the women in the vanguard of each demonstration placed flowers in the gun barrels of the soldiers, called the conscripts their "sons," and were perfectly nonviolent. Some soldiers fired on the crowds, others soon threw down their weapons, removed their uniforms and deserted. Tehran and the other major cities were paralyzed. The main airports were seized, as were the TV and radio stations.

The cry from the crowds was "Allahu Akbar" -- "God is Great." The Khomeini people and mullahs had mobilized God against the Shah.

The Shah deployed armored vehicles: they too were buried in flowers, and the soldiers in them were coerced by the crowds into joining the demonstrations. The country was in chaos and the Shah fled. With his departure the entire edifice of his Imperial government and army vanished, to be replaced at first by the educated Iranians who had gathered around Khomeini in France, who were in turn replaced – having fled into exile - by radicals working for the senior clergy.

In a matter of months the all-powerful edifice of the Shah's government was gone, and by early 1979 the clergy had seized power in his place. This led to the establishment of today's Islamic Republic of Iran, where the senior clergy rules with an iron hand.

As all of this was building to a crescendo I was fortunate in being able to enter into a clandestine relationship with several Iranians who proved to be excellent sources on the plans and intentions of the small crowd of non-religious activists around Khomeini. Their reporting became critical, and for the first time gave us a window into the depth and strength of the anti-Shah rebellion.

Based on these reports and by observing developments in Tehran and around the country, by early 1978 I had developed the very strong opinion that the Shah's days were numbered. This was a view not shared by the COS or his deputy, and when I wrote a long message to Headquarters essentially saying that in my view the Shah's days were finished, the COS refused to send it – stating that it was too pessimistic and "unrealistic." I was thoroughly ticked off by this refusal, but I did not attempt to force the issue – which was a mistake.

Headquarters was much of the same mind as the COS, and it seemed to me that irrespective of our new reporting and what Headquarters could see of events in Iran, the Headquarters analysts were sticking their head in the sand. These analysts, all on the intelligence production side of the Agency, were "old hands" on the subject of Iran. They refused to see in our reporting and in the events on the ground any existential threat to the Shah. I recall a visit by a senior Headquarters analyst who, like his colleagues in the Directorate of Intelligence, was thoroughly skeptical that the events at the time presaged the overthrow of the Shah. I spent some hours talking to him giving him my view of the situation. I'm not sure that my analysis made much difference, but, fortunately for me, a small demonstration against the Embassy took place after we finished our conversation. He told me that did get his attention, and when he left I had the feeling that he was more willing to admit that things might be going very badly wrong in Iran.

After the Shah fell, there were allegations of a huge intelligence failure — blaming both the State Department and the Agency - particularly, as is usual, the Agency. Even though I was swimming upstream inside the Station with my gloomy forecasts of developments, these allegations are not exactly deserved. I am convinced that when this chain of events began, and when the fall of the Shah was much more clearly a possibility, even the Khomeini people did not know that they would succeed. If they didn't know there is no reason in the world why we foreigners would. There is no question in my mind, based on agent reporting, that the whole downward slide of the Shah's Imperial government was in many ways a surprise to those who were working to bring it about. The whole affair started as a small snowball rolling downhill — a snowball which grew to enormous proportions. The disorders that took place following the Shah's collapse were clear evidence that no one was actually in charge.

I attribute the Shah's fall to the fact that so many ordinary Iranians were prepared to take to the streets, frequently risking death at the hands of the Shah's police and/or military, to demonstrate their hatred of the regime. Initially, the demonstrations were largely composed of working-class Iranians — certainly not the college educated elite who were reaping the benefits of the Shah's rule. Once it seemed that his overthrow seemed possible, a fair number of the Shah's erstwhile supporters joined the crowds. Another group that strongly supported the anti-Shah movement was the students in Iran's universities. Some students were particularly radicalized, and they jumped quickly on the religious bandwagon. These so-called students were much more interested in bringing down the Imperial government than actually studying. They are the group that in the Fall of 1979 captured the US Embassy and held it and almost all Embassy personnel hostage for 444 days.

These were difficult days for foreigners in Iran, particularly for Americans, most of who were in Iran on government-related contracts.

# 7

IRAN'S MANEUVERING THROUGH A REVOLUTION

One of the several surprises that greeted me on my arrival in Tehran was the level of security precautions that Embassy personnel and other "official" Americans had to take against assassination. A radical Marxist terrorist organization called the Mujahedeen e-Khalq (MK) had assassinated two senior US military officers several years before. While the MK's principal target was the Shah, it was also focused on Americans. While few in number, the MK posed a real security threat to the many Americans in Tehran, which is where it principally operated.

This meant, for example, that personnel were picked up each day in armored vehicles accompanied by an armed Savak guard. In fact the school buses that picked up our children every day to take them to the very large Department of Defense-run American school had an armed guard aboard. I didn't pay very much attention to the MK at first, but some months into my tour Savak passed the Station information they had obtained after raiding an MK safe house. One of the bits of intelligence found was that several Americans in Tehran had been specifically marked for assassination, and I was one of them. My interest in the MK and its activities increased markedly, and thereafter I carried a pistol for self-defense. It is very unusual for NCS officers to be armed, and permission is only granted by Headquarters and a COS if there is, to quote the famous phrase, a "clear and present danger." I carried a weapon for the next several years in Tehran, and on one occasion I had to make use of it to save my life.

All NCS officers are extensively trained in the use of a variety of firearms – witness our paramilitary and/or defensive security training. However, except for duty in actual war zones, there are very few postings or circumstances where carrying a weapon is advisable or necessary. Few NCS officers have needed to operate while armed.

The NCS view is that if the Service sends people into harm's way where there is a reasonable expectation that they may face a life-threatening situation, they have a right to be armed. Hence we are trained on a contingency basis, and must be "qualified" and "re-qualified" in weapons use through our careers. Every weapons request is carefully reviewed. The fact is that if an officer ever has to draw a weapon he better be prepared to use it – producing a gun is a provocative challenge to any opponent.

Every officer is also trained in what we call "defensive driving." The point of this instruction is to enable one to use his vehicle to escape a terrorist roadblock or attack. We train using actual "clunker" vehicles, and the training can get fairly hair-raising, with both low-speed and high-speed intentional crashes and maneuvers. One technique that is taught is that of moving a car that is blocking you out of the way so that you can make an escape: an interesting technique that can be counterintuitive. And a little scary the first couple of times you do it.

On one occasion in Tehran before the Shah's fall I got caught up in a major demonstration that caused all traffic on one side of a major avenue near the Embassy to be absolutely stopped. There was no traffic on the other side of the median. While I was waiting in my car, hoping the traffic jam would soon end, 10 or 12 young Iranians – who I took to be University students – saw me in my car and proceeded to attack the car with me inside it. They crawled all over the car, and were beating on the windows trying to get at me while I was frozen in place by cars in front and behind me. It was pretty clear that their intention was to drag me from the car and give me a super beating. All this because I clearly looked like I was an American. I was armed, but there was no question of exposing my firearm and using it: there were far too many assailants, and they were not armed. Remembering my training, I used my car as a mini bulldozer, pushing the car front of me out of the way, then backing up a bit so that I could turn and crash over the median strip … dropping off my assailants as I did. I then drove away on the empty side of the avenue. I was lucky to make it home as my intentional crash into the vehicle in front of me had smashed-in the front of my car – which was spewing steam from a broken radiator. I gave thanks that the NCS had sent me through defensive driving school. For certain if I had not been trained in these techniques my assailants would have gotten to me, with unknown but certainly unpleasant consequences.

I later sent a cable to Headquarters recounting the incident, and asked them to inform the appropriate training unit that their hard work had probably saved the life of a case officer. I had to throw the car away, but it had done its job.

I had established my family in a small house immediately adjacent to a large garbage dump. The only redeeming feature of the house was that it had a swimming pool. This was terribly important, since my two sons were largely restricted to the house once they had returned from school each day, and the pool was the source of endless entertainment and fun for them. As a matter of "routine" my wife and I had to be very sensitive and aware of any possible indications of a terrorist attack. This meant paying close attention to the areas around our house – looking for possible surveillance – and being equally careful to look for surveillance when we drove around town. Susan and my boys Colin and Guy, took all of this in stride, which both pleased and greatly relieved me. The thought has occurred to me that most American families in the United States would find a death threat, serious terrorist activity, and the need to employ defensive measures to be a bit much. Not so my troops.

For the first year or so, as I have mentioned above, Iran was a reasonably pleasant place to be – absent the ever-present security dangers. As, however, in 1978 demonstrations and riots began with increasing frequency, we became more and more restricted in when and where we could travel safely. As a result the American "official" community became more and more concerned for the safety of our dependents, and when things really began to heat up there was considerable agitation for the State Department and Department of Defense to evacuate dependents. For months the State Department refused to approve an evacuation, saying, correctly, that the Shah would regard this as a sign that the Americans were pulling out – and thus withdrawing support from him. Things got so grim, however, that some weeks before Christmas, 1978, the State Department acknowledged that the situation in Tehran was growing so difficult that it authorized the departure of wives and children.

State's decision was, in part, the result of a mass demonstration – probably 1000 people – having turned up at the front gate of the Embassy, violently trying to break down the closed gates while throwing rocks and stones inside the compound, plus burning tires and cars on the street in front of the Embassy. For reasons I never quite understood, the Ambassador ordered me to take charge of the Embassy's Marine Guard detail, which was heavily involved in throwing tear gas towards the demonstrators in an attempt to keep them from climbing the wall and/or breaking down the gate. This I did. We soon ran out of teargas, and I called the Ambassador on my radio, telling him that we had no more gas, and that it was therefore likely that the demonstrators would succeed in breaking into the Embassy compound. The Marines were armed, and I told the Ambassador that if we were to keep the crowd out it might be necessary for the Marines to use their firearms. I asked him for instructions: to shoot if necessary or to abandon the defense of the Embassy. He instructed me to shoot if necessary.

I quickly collected my squad of Marines and told them that I would give each one a specific instruction – pat him on the back – to fire if it looked like that was necessary – the decision to use deadly force was mine; this because I did not want the young Marines to open a barrage of fire at the crowd. While we were getting ready to make our "last stand," we heard gunfire coming down the street towards the Embassy. It turned out that a unit of the Shah's Imperial Guard was working its way towards the crowd to disperse them, and was busily firing shots in the air. Faced by a grim and determined looking Army unit, the demonstrators fled. We were all greatly relieved. Later I had to grin, as it was the only time in my life that I was in command of a United States Marine detachment. Perhaps it was the only time in Marine Corps history that an NCS officer commanded Marines.

The State Department chartered a Pan-American 747, onto which nearly 300 children were loaded and shipped off to the United States. I well remember putting tags on the jackets of both boys with the address of their grandparents in Phoenix, Arizona. I had no idea how they would get there – I assumed that State and Headquarters would see to their safe delivery to Phoenix, which they did. My wife refused to leave, and stayed on for several more weeks until the situation was absolutely untenable and I insisted that she depart: which she did with considerable reluctance. She left on one of the sporadic commercial flights that had resumed serving Tehran.

The flight of that chartered Pan Am 747 is illustrative of the chaos that Tehran had sunk into even before the Shah left. The entire airport staff had simply walked off their jobs, so there was no control tower, no customs, no immigration – just an empty terminal. The Pan Am crews were all volunteers, and the only way the aircraft could land was for it to be guided by the Embassy's Air Force Attaché, who sat in his car at one end of the runway and talked the plane in using a hand-held radio.

To back up a bit, as the anti-Shah crescendo built up, the American school was shut down, and everyone who could stayed at home. The nights were particularly threatening as the sound of gunfire became more common, and each night featured people all over our neighborhoods going to their rooftops to shout "Allahhu Akbar" – the anti-Shah catchphrase. Much of this noise, we later learned, was staged by the anti-Shah people, who would broadcast recordings of gunfire and the "God is Great" chants. But a fair amount of it was real as the increasingly well-armed anti-Shah people took on the Shah's police and military in battles around the city.

In anticipation of the house either being attacked or being struck by stray bullets, I prepared a "safe room" in the basement of the house, well away from the street. We laid down mattresses on the floor of the room, and for a good many nights the boys and my wife would bed down in the room, as I would when I was not working. One night we did have several rounds fired into the house – not, I was certain, intentionally… just stray bullets. One of which I have framed and I am looking at as I write. I was and am terribly proud of the boys and Susan for keeping their cool. Guy was seven, and Colin was 10: neither of them complained. I shall never forget the boys, after their evening showers, in their pajamas and bathrobes, filing down into our safe haven, where we sat in darkness until the shooting died down. Only once, in the course of a particularly noisy night, did Guy admit to being "a little frightened." I hugged him, and it was hard not to have tears come to my eyes. He and Colin were evacuated several days later.

I remember an amusing incident that involved Susan and one of the Shah's armored vehicles. A tank had driven up and parked directly in front of our garage door, blocking our car in. Susan opened the door, discovered the tank, saw she could not drive out of the garage, and got indignant. She banged on the hull of the tank until the hatch opened and a head emerged. Since she had pretty good Farsi by this time she asked the driver "whose tank is this?" The soldier meekly acknowledged that it was his. Susan then told him in no uncertain terms that he was to move his tank forward 30 meters and stop blocking our driveway, which he did.

Immediately after the Shah left the country things came to a head: the Army collapsed, with the exception of the Shah's Imperial Guard, which held out until the very end. The conscript Army had essentially abandoned its weapons and gone home and their weapons were now in the hands of the Khomeini people. Old scores were being settled all over the country, and Tehran television now regularly featured photographs of former Imperial Iranian Army and Savak officers on mortuary slabs. The Shah's Prime Minister was executed in his home. Every senior Iranian official under the Shah had to get out of the country or risk death, and many were killed before they could escape.

Ayatollah Khomeini quickly set up a rump government, in the main led by non-clerics who had been with him in exile in France. By and large these were reasonable men, who in their turn would be devoured by the revolution. But they did give us someone to work with during the chaos of the first months following the Shah's departure.

Things came to a head on Valentine's Day of 1979, when a large crowd of heavily armed Iranians attacked and literally shot their way into the Embassy, capturing the entire embassy staff, blindfolding some and tying the hands of many others. It was a minor wonder that no Americans were killed in the process of taking the Embassy over, and take it over they did. The Embassy screamed for help from the newly established "provisional government," and at the end of the day the entire staff was freed. But... and this is a big but... the people who had attacked the Embassy remained there, and from that day forward controlled all movement into and <u>inside</u> the Embassy compound. The Embassy occupied a full city block, which under normal diplomatic rules of behavior would be considered to have complete diplomatic immunity. It was just crazy that the compound was now patrolled <u>internally</u> by armed Iranian thugs – people I called the butcher, the baker and the candlestick maker. They went freely anywhere they wanted to. They controlled all access to the compound, and were a surly bunch, only very reluctantly acceding to the constraints placed on them by the interim government. I suspect that if they had had their way they would have shot the entire Embassy staff. This situation continued until my departure in, as I recall, May or June 1979.

As part of capturing the Embassy many offices were literally shot up: there were bullet holes in the windows and walls, and all desks were ransacked and anything of value stolen. All the classified material in the Embassy had been destroyed before this attack, which with typical American humor came to be called the "St. Valentine's Day massacre." Again, thanks to the efforts of the moderates in the interim government, no American personnel continued to be held hostage.

In the wake of the capture of the Embassy, the State Department ordered all nonessential US government personnel to leave Iran, which meant that only a handful of people would remain. With this instruction there began the withdrawal of virtually all Americans from the country, and, with the help of the interim government, thousands of Americans, breadwinners and their dependents, left Iran. It seemed like a logical step since the Embassy was in "enemy" hands, and all contracts between US defense firms and the Shah's government were effectively canceled and their personnel withdrawn.

At this point, Ambassador William Sullivan, one of the great men of the American Foreign Service, ordered both the COS and his Deputy to leave the country, accompanied by virtually all other Station personnel. The White House, however, directly ordered Headquarters to keep a small station in existence in Iran, and I was named Acting Chief of Station.

Thus began one of the wilder periods of my life. I remember saying to myself, as I watched most of the Embassy staff departing the compound under an armed escort from our hostile "protectors," that *this was the moment that all my training and time in the Service had prepared me for.*

I kept a handful of officers, and we began to provide the only reporting from American sources in Iran. The handful of State Department officers who remained did not, of course, have anyone to talk to except the new provisional government, so the burden of informing Washington on what was happening fell principally into our hands. We continued to be in contact with our remaining sources, and began submitting a stream of intelligence reporting to Washington. I was very proud of my handful of junior officers who, as almost all other Americans had literally left the country, professionally carried on with their jobs. We continued to operate under the most trying of conditions; occasional gun battles were still taking place around the city, and all Americans who remained in the country were considered to be spies. And therefore they were potentially subject to every sort of arbitrary "justice" at the hands of the vengeful and newly empowered Khomeini supporters, who had turned themselves into vigilantes hunting down former key Shah supporters and, of course, "spies," particularly American.

I felt very responsible for the young officers who stayed in Iran with me, and did everything I could to minimize the risks that they were taking. They had guts, but we needed luck and caution to do our jobs and stay alive. We had the keys to hundreds of now-empty houses, and hundreds of abandoned vehicles. All of us moved from empty house to empty house using the most dilapidated and inconspicuous cars from our fleet of vehicles. We kept in contact with each other through secure radios, and all of our reporting to Washington was done using emergency procedures. My case officers would report to me over secure radios, I would review the reporting and send it on to Washington. In addition to agent reporting, we forwarded our own observations on what was happening to Headquarters. As a practical matter we were actually operating in a wartime situation in an enemy-held city, and every meeting with an agent – and in fact just moving about the city – was fraught with danger. Not for the first or last time in my career I wished I was not a large blonde haired, blued-eyed guy who stood out in the local crowd.

There were some nasty incidents during this period. On one occasion I was stopped in my car by a small crowd of heavily armed Iranians: obviously the "armed defenders of the revolution" from a mosque in the neighborhood. I was physically removed from my car, and at gunpoint ordered to stand against the wall, while being called a CIA spy. One Iranian who could speak English translated for me, and it was clear that I was being subjected to a drumhead trial. After an hour's harangue I was told that I was going to be executed. I protested my innocence to no avail, and it began to look to me that my life would end up against a wall in downtown Tehran. I asked for a mullah, and a messenger was duly sent away to bring one back. We waited for about an hour until a young man in clerical garb turned up. My captors had a long conversation with him in Farsi; the only words of which I could understand were "CIA" and "spy." Through the English-speaking captor I asked to speak to the mullah, at which point I earnestly reminded him that the Quran forbade murder, which was clearly what my captors had in mind. To my enormous relief he apparently agreed, and he instructed the crowd to let me loose. I don't know, of course, if my captors actually would have shot me: it sure as hell looked like they would. I gave my sincere thanks to that young mullah, climbed in my car and headed off to hide in some safe house for the night.

It is a frightening experience to be tried and sentenced to death, and I don't recommend it.

This incident heightened my concern for my officers, and I was determined to get them out of Iran. Headquarters agreed, and one by one my guys were able to get on airplanes and leave the country. I saw no purpose in offering up case officers to the mob, particularly as fewer and fewer of our agent assets remained in the country and there was increasingly little for my officers to do. As I recall, I was able to have all the case officers under my command depart the country before I did.

There was one other incident in which I was involved. I had to make a clandestine agent meeting in a car very late at night with an

Iranian official who had been a reporting source. He was in hiding, and quite correctly feared for his life. It was necessary for me to give him an alias passport and provide him with money to escape the country. That meeting being successfully over, I turned the corner and ran directly into a roadblock. This time I was dragged from my car by two Iranian thugs who also called me a CIA spy, knocked me to the ground, and proceeded to try to beat me to death with their heavy boots and rifle butts. I was very badly hurt, and there was no question this time that it was their intention to kill me. I was armed and was able to get a couple of shots off and escape.

I did not report either of these events to Headquarters, as I was concerned that if I did they might order me to depart Iran – leaving my young officers on their own. I did confide in Ken Haas, my senior subordinate, and he agreed with my course of action. Since we did not see each other very often, but maintained contact by secure radio, my bumps and bruises were not evident.

As a sad footnote to this time in Tehran, Ken and a number of other American personnel were killed in a savage terrorist attack which blew up the American Embassy in Beirut. This was a tragic end for a brilliant and promising officer, who left a lovely wife and children.

The time came for me to leave the country in the early summer of 1979, and as one of my last official acts as Chief of Station I wrote a message to Headquarters saying that I believed that another attack on Americans was highly likely, and that I thought that it would be foolhardy to attempt to build a Station back up again. I ended with a recommendation that once I was withdrawn no additional CIA personnel should be sent to Iran for the foreseeable future. I showed this message to Ambassador Sullivan, and asked him to comment on it before I sent it to Washington. He agreed with what I had to say, so the last line of the message was very brief: "Ambassador Concurs."

In retrospect I was right. Unfortunately, both the State Department and CIA soon began to rebuild a Station and Embassy – some of whom were taken hostage in October 1979 and held for 444 days. This rebuilding precipitated the "Iran hostage crisis" that saw the ill-fated Iran Hostage Rescue Mission that probably ended the Jimmy Carter presidency.

I have never understood President Carter's decisions regarding Iran. It seemed to me that any sensible president would simply have withdrawn the entire American official presence in Iran until things settled down. I am fairly certain that was Ambassador Sullivan's opinion as well. I know that Sullivan was having frequent arguments with the President's National Security Advisor, Zbigniew Brezinski, over the issue, and I suspect that Zbig was the driving force behind the President's order to keep an Embassy open and to re-staff it as soon as possible.

The consequences of this decision – which I thought at the time was pure stupidity – became all too clear in October 1979, when the US Embassy was again attacked and personnel taken hostage.

It was a decision that threw the United States into a crisis.

8

THE IRAN RESCUE MISSION

By the time I was instructed to leave Tehran and return to Headquarters some sense of normality had returned to Tehran. The airport was back in business and, considering what had been going on for the previous months; Tehran was almost an oasis of calm. A number of Americans were on a Pan Am flight for Europe and the States: boarding was much muted, and for the first hour or so the passengers were deadly silent. Then the aircraft captain came on the loudspeaker: "ladies and gentlemen, we have just left Iranian airspace." The passengers burst into spontaneous applause. The flight attendants passed out free drinks, and the entire atmosphere inside the airplane changed. Such was the relief to leave Iran.

I reported immediately to Headquarters and was told to "take a few weeks of leave." No one appeared to have the slightest interest in debriefing me, so I immediately collected my family – now reunited after a spell in Arizona – and we went down to our home on top of the Blue Ridge Mountains. The following weeks were absolutely idyllic, passed all too quickly, and ended with my return to Headquarters and a new assignment to a Headquarters Branch. I expected to be at Headquarters for a two-year tour before my next assignment, which was an unknown. The boys settled into their new school and it looked like the rest of 1979 was going to pass uneventfully.

Once again, however, Iran raised its ugly head. In October 1979, "radical students" stormed the Embassy and took prisoner the 53 American diplomatic personnel who happened to be on the Embassy grounds. The new government of Iran asserted that it was helpless to end this new violation and it quickly became evident that our hostages were being held with the full consent of the Ayatollah Khomeini, who was by now the "paramount power" in Iran. Protests by Washington fell on deaf ears, and it was apparent that the "students" intended to hold their American prisoners indefinitely.

In a situation like this, a clear violation of all international laws, the President of the United States should have taken immediate and firm action to obtain the release of the hostages. In my view this was a relatively straightforward matter: a quiet message would be sent to the Iranians that unless the Americans were released immediately, American aircraft would attack the vulnerable Iranian petroleum facilities in the south of the country. Since Iran's only income came from the export of petroleum, such an act would pose a grave and unacceptable threat to the Iranian economy. President Jimmy Carter, whose naïveté in foreign affairs was already shockingly evident, elected not to take this course of action. Why we will never know. The seizure of our Embassy was tantamount to a declaration of war, and Iran's claim that these "students" were acting independently of the Government of Iran and were thus beyond the government's control, were patently fraudulent. This set in motion the major crisis of Jimmy Carter's presidency, since while Carter apparently wrung his hands and did nothing that would persuade the Iranian government to release the hostages, the world watched in disbelief as the United States knuckled under to the Ayatollah.

I am as sure as it is possible to be that had Carter made the above threat – secretly, in order not to cause the Iranian government to lose face – the hostages would have been freed. Instead, Carter continued to wring his hands, and in the end our hostages were kept for 444 days, until Ronald Reagan entered the White House. A superpower was humbled by a ragtag bunch of so-called "students" supported by a clerical Muslim government that had just come to power in a country that was still recovering from a revolution. To those of us who knew Iran well, Carter's position was absolutely shocking. To this day I do not understand why Carter did not respond to force with the threat of using force, which we had in abundance.

Instead of doing the obvious, in the deepest secrecy Carter instructed the Department of Defense and the Central intelligence Agency to attempt to plan a rescue mission to extricate our hostages from Iran.

Since I had just returned from Iran, I was called in by my Division chief, Chuck Cogan, and told that I would be the senior CIA liaison officer with the Pentagon in attempting to plan such a rescue mission. I was deeply honored to be given this job by Chuck, a man I much admired for his thoughtful approach to difficult problems and low key personality. As a brand new GS-15 (the military equivalent of Colonel) I was relatively young for my new assignment, and I very much appreciated his having given me the job. As the years went on Chuck would have considerable influence on my professional life, and it was a real pleasure to work for him. Some people mistook Chuck's laid-back and quiet demeanor to suggest that he lacked "fire in his belly." Nothing could be further from the truth. Chuck was a highly competent and thoughtful senior officer who just happened to have a quiet approach to problems and issues — a refreshing change from his bombastic predecessor.

Thus began the next chapter in my relationship with Iran. On the face of it, attempting a rescue mission into the heart of Tehran was impossible. Over time it moved from being impossible to, with luck, being just barely possible.

At my first meeting at the Pentagon, I met Maj. Gen. Jim Vaught, who had been designated by the Chairman of the Joint Chiefs of Staff to lead the secret Pentagon Task Force planning the mission, and to execute the mission if a plan could be developed and the President so ordered. Jim Vaught and I turned out to make an excellent team. He ran all the military elements of the proposed rescue mission, and I was his senior intelligence advisor and the coordinator of all intelligence activities in support of the mission. Jim was from Georgia, and behind his gracious "good old Georgia boy" façade there was a keen and agile mind. We developed a close collegial relationship: I stayed out of military matters and he looked to me on the intelligence side.

Our ground rules were simple: absolutely no one was to be made aware of the existence of this new "task force," much less its purpose, unless it was absolutely necessary. Everyone who was brought into the operation was sworn to total secrecy. In the military, only the Joint Chiefs of Staff were aware of the plan. At Headquarters, only the Director, Adm. Stansfield Turner; and Chuck Cogan, in whose Area Division Iran fell, were initially aware of the project. Cogan set up a completely compartmented office to deal with the project from the Agency perspective: all communications and activities would eventually flow through this Headquarters "war room."

The scope of the project was extraordinary: by the time the mission was run, hundreds of CIA people had been brought in to perform specific tasks in support of the operation – and they did it without knowing exactly why they were doing what they did. The same thing was true for the military. For once "compartmentation" worked. By the President's directive, no one in the State Department, including Secretary of State Cyrus Vance himself, was apprised of the plan. (Vance did not know about it until the day it failed. He was furious, and he immediately resigned.)

The military side of the rescue mission has been told in several books so I will gloss over all but the most important aspects of the rescue attempt. The single best book on the mission, in my opinion, is, *"The Iranian Rescue Mission – Why it Failed,"* by Paul B. Ryan, The Naval Institute Press, 1985.

What has not been revealed heretofore is the role that CIA played in making the mission possible. While the mission itself was aborted on the ground at the last minute, without CIA support it could not possibly have been attempted. In the end, in terms of building a complex, multi-faceted capability it was a brilliant day for CIA and the other intelligence agencies (like NSA) that supported our activities.

From the beginning, it was clear that CIA's role in any possible rescue mission was not going to be limited to providing intelligence information to the military. Yes, CIA would provide intelligence; but it also would have a direct role in designing the final plan for the mission; and would provide operational capabilities to make attempting the mission possible. This point is worth stressing: there exists within CIA all manner of skills, resources, and capabilities that were needed in the rescue operation. Everything from analyzing satellite photography, monitoring Iranian radio communications, providing false documentation, producing "all source finished intelligence" reporting and building communications equipment **was done**. In a sense, CIA is and was a huge "tool and parts box" from which we could draw absolutely indispensable support.

At the end of the day it was CIA's responsibility to clandestinely deliver the hostage rescue force to the Embassy compound.

As the senior intelligence guy for the mission, my role was twofold: to design a complex intelligence and operational support "package" for the mission, and to make sure that the many different pieces of that package meshed. Many elements within the NCS and the Agency as a whole were involved throughout the stages of planning and mounting the mission. For six months, from late October 1979 until late April 1980 all facets of our support to the military consumed me utterly.

Our first action was to move the Army's brand-new hostage rescue force - code-named Delta - to a secure CIA facility. The idea was to get Delta, whose existence at the time was a closely held secret, away from its normal base at Fort Bragg in North Carolina to where it could be supported without triggering any interest from the "regular" Army. Delta would end up spending many months under the CIA's wing, and CIA provided the unit with everything from quarters and rations to firing ranges to an endless supply of ammunition. This was a necessary step, as Delta simply disappeared from view.

The biggest question before the planners was how to get from outside Iran to the American Embassy in Tehran, kill the guard force, retrieve the hostages, leave the Embassy and exit Iran. No small issue considering that many thousands of miles would have to be covered. It was quickly decided that any rescue operation would ultimately depend on having helicopters to lift Delta Force and the rescued hostages out of the Embassy to some airfield where large transport aircraft could pick up all these people and get them out of the country, leaving the helicopters behind.

CIA paramilitary officers provided the first part of the complex puzzle that came to constitute the rescue plan. They came up with the idea of launching the helicopters from a Navy aircraft carrier well offshore Iran, with the helicopters flying deep into the country (600 nautical miles) and landing on a stretch of road in the middle of the

Iranian desert. That stretch of road (labeled "Desert One") would become a landing strip for large C-130 transport aircraft that would bring Delta and associated elements into Iran to rendezvous with helicopters. The C-130s would also provide fuel for the helicopters, which would arrive at the desert strip with empty tanks. Once Delta was "mated" to the helicopters on Night One of the "insertion" into Iran, the C-130s would exit Iran, and the helicopters and Delta would hide out for the next day. On the Night Two a fleet of CIA-provided trucks would carry Delta to the wall of the Embassy, which would allow the force to surprise the Iranian guards and rescue the hostages. That same night the helicopters would fly from their concealed positions in the desert to the Embassy compound and lift Delta and the rescued hostages out. The helicopters would then fly to a remote airfield not far from Tehran, which would have been captured by a unit of US Army Rangers. C-141 transports would fly into this remote airfield and rendezvous with the helicopters. All hands – Delta, the freed hostages, the Army Rangers and the helicopter crews would all depart the country on the C-141s, blowing up the abandoned helicopters.

If that sounds hellishly complicated, it was. Every part of the plan had to work flawlessly. Once the plan had been adopted, myriad intelligence requirements had to be met, and this is where CIA showed its mettle.

First was the matter of seeing whether the stretch of road that CIA had identified as "Desert One" was strong enough to bear the weight of heavily laden C-130 transports. In order to satisfy this requirement, a small CIA aircraft flew deep into Iran and landed at Desert One. Aboard was a US Air Force technician who, with his equipment, could test the roadbed to see if it met load-bearing requirements. That flight was a success, the road proved adequate to take the weight of the transports, and the aircraft successfully entered and exited Iran without detection.

Second, a small fleet of trucks had to be obtained to carry Delta from the desert to the Embassy. This was an absolutely crucial part of the overall plan: only by having Delta arrive together, undetected, and delivered to the Embassy wall in secrecy could the operation have possibly succeeded. The trucks were as indispensable a part of the mission as were the helicopters. This involved CIA procuring a number of brand-new Mercedes "tractors" – in Iran – which would pull brand-new trailers containing Delta. Delta drew up the plans for the trailers, and CIA agents in Tehran purchased the truck/tractors and had the trailers built – again in Tehran – to Delta's specifications. This was an absolutely brilliant piece of work.

When the night came these trucks were parked in the desert at the rendezvous point, hubcap to hubcap, ready to cover the roughly 60 remaining miles to the Embassy in downtown Tehran.

It was also necessary to have Iranian drivers for the trucks, as it was likely that the trucks would be stopped at one or more checkpoints along the long road between the rendezvous point and the Embassy: it was essential that an Iranian driver in each truck be prepared to deal with guards at these checkpoints. CIA recruited a group of Iranians – none of whom had a clue of how to drive a tractor-trailer rig – and put them through an intensive course in how to drive the "sixteen wheeler" rigs. These agents, once trained, had to be sequestered until the mission. In fact they only learned what they were going to be doing when I informed them on an airplane far from the United States and on the way to Iran. They were a brave bunch, and they did not bat an eye when they learned what their mission would be. They, too, would be withdrawn in the helicopters from the Embassy.

Next, it was necessary to establish surveillance on the Embassy compound in order that we might be sure that the resident guard force was not unexpectedly reinforced before the night of the mission. The military was adamant that these had to be "American eyes" on the compound. This requirement was met.

One of the most difficult requirements given to us by Delta was to identify where each hostage was in the many buildings on the Embassy compound. For a long time this seemed to be an impossible requirement, as it could only be filled by someone who was operating in the compound: by definition one of the hostage keepers. While we tried mightily to obtain this information it did not look like we would be able to, which would mean that Delta would have to search all the buildings in the Embassy compound. At the last moment, we came up with the information, and the night before the mission began we were able to brief Delta on where each hostage was kept. Nothing could have been more important, since that information would save the soldiers from Delta a great deal of time, and time, once inside the compound, was of the essence.

There were myriad other requirements. To name a few:

- ❖ Flying from the aircraft carrier USS Nimitz over 600 miles of Iranian desert, the helicopters had to arrive at a small spot on a road many miles from Tehran. Navigation could and would be a problem, and the Agency stepped up to help solve it by providing an inertial navigation system. Once again the military did not have this sort of sophisticated navigation aid, which CIA had developed to enable it to carry out "deep penetration missions" very similar to this one. This system enables a pilot to start from a known position and end up at another known position. Today such equipment is standard issue, but in 1979 it was an unheard-of technological breakthrough.
- ❖ The Navy and Marine Corps helicopter pilots involved in the mission had never envisaged flying at night and landing without lights. Several sets of crews were vetted and trained at the CIA secret facility, and several sets washed out because of their inability to land in the dark without lights. CIA paramilitary officers, some of whom were helicopter pilots who had trained in "no lights" operations, were called in to assist in training the military aviators. Our use of infrared lighting was demonstrated and adopted by the military.
- ❖ Delta needed a scale model of the Embassy compound so that all teams, once they were in the compound, would know how to negotiate it. The model had to be absolutely correct and to scale, and a CIA office built the necessary model.

When ordered by President Carter to execute the mission on 24 April 1980, I was startled when General Vaught told me of his intention to remain at the forward staging base in Egypt from which we launched the rescue attempt. To me this meant that the three Colonels on the ground at Desert One, each of whom commanded a different constituent part of the overall force (Beckwith/Delta; Jim Kyle/Air Force; and the Navy/ helicopter unit commander) would not have an officer senior to them at Desert One. I knew that General Vaught had appointed Col. Kyle to be the "commander on the ground," but I thought that this could be a potential problem, particularly because I knew Charlie Beckwith would dominate the trio. I said this to Jim very deferentially, as again it was not within my purview to comment on strictly military matters. He told me he was confident, because of satellite radio communications, that his not being at Desert One <u>would not</u> be a problem, and that he would be of most use in Egypt, where he would have direct contact with the Pentagon.

With hindsight, it was a problem. This brings me to Colonel Charlie Beckwith, the founder and first commanding officer of Delta. Charlie was a big, bluff, outrageously outspoken combat soldier with a remarkable Vietnam War record. His courage was legendary. He had fashioned Delta in an image that he had largely created. His troops adored him, and his officers, while competent, were his acolytes. I did not share their view. I often had the feeling in the months leading up to the mission, when a noisy Charlie Beckwith constantly berated CIA for never giving him "enough" intelligence, that Charlie was too protective of "his" Delta force. I was not alone in my concern that Charlie, who had done a fine job in raising Delta, might be inadequate to the task of taking it on its first and most important mission. Jim Vaught also had his concerns, some of which he shared with me. I was asked directly by a member of the Joint Chiefs of Staff if I thought Beckwith was the right man to command Delta on the rescue mission. I replied that I did <u>not</u> think so, but – and here was the problem – to remove Charlie before the mission might have been a morale-breaker in Delta. He agreed. It seemed to me that Charlie's superiors were not happy with his performance, but that the issue of morale in Delta force was of such great concern that they did not dare to replace him on the eve of its first operational deployment.

The mission was aborted at Desert One because Beckwith insisted that an insufficient number of helicopters were still capable of making the onward trip: of the eight helicopters launched from the aircraft carrier, one had turned back, one had force-landed on the way towards Desert One, was abandoned and its crew transferred to another helicopter, and the third, while it made it to the desert rendezvous, was deemed unfit for further service – leaving only five working helicopters. Col. Beckwith insisted that <u>six helicopters</u> had to be available for the mission to go forward. This was a questionable assertion, since five - probably even four - helicopters could have carried all the people involved, but Beckwith's insistence on having six "birds" prevailed, and it was decided to abort the mission.

This seemed to some of us to have been a very incorrect decision, as some things must be left to chance. But the determined Col. Beckwith had his way. The planes were ordered to leave Iran.

At this point the mission changed from a failure to a tragedy. One helicopter took off from behind a C-130 transport from which it had just been refueled, and, in the clouds of dust that surrounded the entire landing area, the pilot mistakenly flew forward (instead of up and backward) and struck the C-130 – which burst into flames. With aircraft parked wingtip to wingtip, the flames and accompanying explosions spread rapidly, and, in the end, eight helicopter aircrew members were killed in the ensuing fires.

The bodies of these burned-to-death airmen were later transferred to the "students" holding our Embassy in Tehran, where the corpses were brutalized by them and a mob. Such was the nature of the Embassy captors.

It was several years before I could find the strength to visit Arlington National Cemetery to see the monument to these eight airmen.

A few vignettes from the operation:

- ❖ Prior to leaving Headquarters for Egypt, where from a remote airbase in the desert the entire mission would be launched, I was ordered to report to the Deputy Director of Central Intelligence, then Frank Carlucci, who asked me whether I thought that we could actually rescue the hostages. My reply was that <u>if the helicopters worked</u> on the various "legs" of the mission I thought we had an even chance of success. I also told him that in what was supposed to be a dress rehearsal for the raid, helicopters flying a shorter distance than was involved in Iran did <u>not</u> arrive as scheduled. The Navy's excuse for this was that the helicopters they used, while identical to those that were now on the USS Nimitz, were not "as good" as the ones now on the carrier. I told him that I had total confidence in the US Air Force's very large role in in the mission — but that the helicopters were absolutely our Achilles' heel. Carlucci shook his head and wished me luck.

❖ Early in the mission planning it was decided by the Joint Chiefs of Staff that Navy helicopters would be used for the mission. Apparently the justification for this was that since the aircraft would be launched from a Navy carrier the helicopters had to be Marine and Navy machines. When I learned this from General Vaught I was surprised. Not only were the Navy helicopters not air-refuelable (which would have made an enormous difference in our mission planning, and greatly eased the problems of keeping the helicopters operational), but their crews had not been trained in any sort of covert long-distance penetration missions into enemy territory. I was aware that the Air Force had a contingent of the same type of helicopters that had been modified for air refueling, and whose crews consistently trained in the kind of missions that we would fly in Iran. I told Jim it seemed to me to be absurd not to use the best equipment and crews we had, and that the Air Force unit filled the bill. He agreed, but stated that he had been forced to accept the JCS decision. This caused no end of problems. The Navy found it very difficult to find helicopter pilots who could fly the kind of nighttime, unorthodox mission they were being called on to perform. As I recall we went through three complete sets of pilots before "adequate" personnel were selected. Second, the fact that the Navy helicopters were not air-refuelable meant that the Air Force would have to refuel all of the helicopters at Desert One, flying in C-130 tankers to do the job. Bitter inter-service rivalry had raised its ugly head, and this decision would come back to haunt us.

❖ The night before we lifted out of Egypt to commence the raid, CIA had, as I have previously noted, determined where all the hostages were located inside the compound. This last-minute information was a godsend to Delta, and resulted in some juggling of Delta's team assignments. With this information in hand it was clear that even Beckwith believed that we had an enormously improved chance of rescuing the hostages. At that moment I believed that <u>if the helicopters worked</u>, CIA would play its role and deliver Delta to the compound in absolute secrecy in the dead of night. And that, with the hostage locations known, Delta would succeed in overwhelming the guard force and collecting the hostages for the helicopter evacuation.

- ❖ After all final arrangements had been made there was a very dramatic ceremony in the aircraft hangar where Delta was gathered. Someone read the 23rd Psalm. Then the entire group sang "God bless America." There were more than a few tears in some very tough men's eyes. I want to stress that every single person on the mission was quite prepared to give his life in order to rescue the 53 hostages. It seemed to us that the United States had been so humiliated, and our people so abused, that this was a God-given opportunity to rectify a terrible wrong.

- ❖ An amusing incident happened just before the mission was launched. I climbed aboard a C-141 to find a large number of boxes strapped down on the floor, and six or eight men in U.S. Army uniforms, all Colonels, just lounging around. I asked who they were: it turned out they were Army doctors of a very special kind. They had put their names down to be available for any mission, anytime, anywhere. They had unceremoniously been ordered aboard an aircraft filled with medical equipment and flown off to Egypt. They didn't have a clue where they were or what they were supposed to be doing, and apparently had been absolutely forgotten. I introduced myself as a "CIA guy," and filled them in on the mission. Their job would be to fly several thousand miles into the Iranian air base that the US Army Rangers were to capture, to provide medical assistance to what we assumed would be a fair number of casualties from the Embassy raid. They heard me out in stunned silence. Then, to their credit, they grinned and said "okay ... let's get to work," which they did by opening up the boxes and breaking out their medical equipment. Quite a change, said one of the doctors, from delivering babies at Fort Something-or-other. Neat guys.

❖ Since it was my job to orchestrate all of the many CIA contributions to the mission, and since we, in fact, would have complete responsibility for delivering Delta to the Embassy, I felt it necessary to accompany the mission if and when it was deployed. I intentionally waited until we had received word to launch the mission before asking for the necessary approval to accompany it. In a teletype "conversation" with the Director, Admiral Turner, from the Egyptian forward operations base just prior to launch, I asked Turner to make sure that I had formal "operational orders" to proceed into Iran. (These were necessary, for if I just disappeared on the mission without formal orders the bureaucrats in Washington could simply say that I had "vanished." In order to protect my family – so they would get survivor benefits in the event of my death – I had to be on official orders.) The request clearly surprised the Admiral, who, as I expected, at first objected to my going on the mission at all. I explained to him that hundreds of lives were at stake, all of which were relying on CIA's arrangements and resources: it seemed to me that if we were confident in those arrangements we should prove that by my going along with the mission. Besides, I might be able to contribute some "local knowledge" during the raid. He agreed, and instructed that orders be issued for me to enter Iran – albeit with some rather unusual travel arrangements.

❖ At that last meeting in Egypt one of the soldiers from Delta approached me with an American flag tied around his waist. He asked me "Mr. Hart, where shall I put the flag." He obviously very rightly wanted to leave an American flag flying at the Embassy. I walked him through a location where the flag would be sure to be seen from the street outside the compound. My instructions were for him to enter the Ambassador's Residence (which was his assigned target) and go to the second floor by using the main stairway. Directly in front of him would be the door to the Ambassador's bedroom, on the far side of which was doors leading to a balcony. By hanging the flag on the top rail of the balcony it would be clearly visible from the street. Assuming the raid was a success, the world press – including all the American networks and CNN – would no doubt be all around the Embassy compound, and would see the American flag in place. After the disaster at Desert One, I helped the same soldier board the aircraft I was in. As I helped pull him up through the door into the airplane he saw who I was, and he said in a broken voice "Sir ... I'm sorry about the flag." I was moved near to tears.

On our return to the staging base in Egypt I met with a grimly depressed General Vaught. I told him that I thought that the mission could have worked, but it was clear that God and Lady Luck were not with us in Iran.

I then walked some yards away from the command bunker, sat down and wept. All I could think of was my poor – soon to be disappointed – country.

In retrospect, it seems clear that the one thing that might have saved the mission from its catastrophic failure would have been a full-blown dress rehearsal in the United States. This was never attempted, why I do not know. We certainly had plenty of time to conduct such an exercise, and had we done so many problems, large and small, that later surfaced would have been detected.

For example, the Air Force never deployed the fleet of C-130 aircraft that landed at Desert One on an equivalent road in an equivalent desert in the US. Had it done so it would have found that leaving the engines on all the aircraft running while sitting on the ground created a major dust storm that both limited visibility and risked clogging aircraft engines. A full dress rehearsal would have included having eight helicopters land behind the C-130s, and again the hellish problem of a machine-created dust storm would have been evident; to say nothing of determining with more precision the question of helicopter survivability in a desert environment. There were also serious problems of communication between the units, and command and control issues – these too would have become evident.

A Life for A Life

This, of course, is hindsight, but I consider it to be the most significant factor in the eventual failure of the mission. A full dress rehearsal would have either proven the mission to be impractical or enabled us to fine tune the operation to give it a vastly greater chance of success. There was no lack of courage and determination on the part of hundreds of people, but courage alone very often will not win the day.

While the rescue attempt was aborted by the military on the ground in Iran because of problems with helicopters, every part of the Agency's role in the mission was accomplished successfully due to the dedication, hard work and competence of all the various people and Agency elements involved. I still believe that only CIA, with its extraordinary range of specialties and people, could have handled the job.

In the end, my brave band of Iranian truck drivers emerged unscathed, as did all the other elements of the mission ... but for the eight aircrew who died at Desert One.

9

ISLAMABAD, PAKISTAN: THE AFGHAN WAR

"In January 1984, CIA director William Casey briefed President Reagan and his national security cabinet about the progress of their covert Afghan war. Mujahedin warriors had killed or wounded about 17,000 Soviet soldiers to date, by the CIA's classified estimate. They controlled 62% of the countryside and had become so effective that the Soviets would have to triple or quadruple their deployments in Afghanistan to put the rebellion down. Soviet forces had so far lost about 350 to 400 aircraft in combat, the CIA estimated. Mujahedin had also destroyed about 2750 Soviet tanks and armored carriers, and just under 8000 trucks, jeeps, and other vehicles. The war had already cost the Soviet government about $12 billion in direct expenses. All this mayhem had been purchased by US taxpayers for $200 million so far, plus another $200 million contributed by (the Saudi's), Casey reported."[1]

When Director Casey made the above presentation to President Reagan I had completed 2 ½ years of my three-year tour in Islamabad. In a way this "battle damage assessment" serves as my report card.

And therein hangs the tale.

After the Iran rescue mission, I returned to my normal duties at Headquarters, in this case as chief of the Afghanistan Branch. The Soviets had invaded Afghanistan in December 1979. This was the first

---

[1] From Ghost Wars: The Secret History of the CIA, Afghanistan, and Bin Laden, from the Soviet Invasion to September 10, 2001, Steven Coll, Penguin Books, December 28, 2004.

flat-out Soviet invasion of another country since the Soviets had moved in to suppress the Hungarian revolution in 1956, and was actually the first Soviet full-force military movement outside of the Communist Bloc since the end of World War II.

In early 1980, a timid CIA had requested President Jimmy Carter's approval of a very limited program to assist the Afghan insurgents by providing medical supplies: strictly non-lethal equipment. Carter had approved the measure, but this token gesture was nothing more than a drop in the bucket as far as the fledgling insurgency inside Afghanistan was concerned. The Pakistanis had indicated an interest in helping the Afghan insurgents, but Headquarters was not convinced that the Pakistanis were serious; that the Afghan insurgents were a credible threat to the Soviets; or that there would be any support for a covert program in the Carter White House.

I was sent to Pakistan in the early summer of 1981, an assignment I very much coveted and was extremely pleased to receive. South Asia was my first interest in terms of assignments, and I had already done five years there. I had long been a student of the history of the tribes along the Pakistan–Afghan border, particularly of the endless battles between British Indian Army forces and the wildly unruly Pathans of the largely undefined border between what was then British India and Afghanistan. British India had invaded Afghanistan on several occasions, always coming out on the losing end, and I had a sense that the Soviet Union might have fallen into a far deeper pit than it realized.

Circumstances had changed at Headquarters and in Washington since our initial rather petty bit of non-lethal assistance to the Afghan insurgents. President Reagan had replaced Jimmy Carter, and at Headquarters William Casey, an old World War II OSS hand, had taken over as Director of Central Intelligence. In addition, Chuck Cogan was the Area Division Chief in whose sphere Afghanistan and Pakistan both fell. Further, an old friend and highly competent officer, John McGaffin, headed Headquarters support for the Pakistan project.

Cogan's instructions to me as I left for Pakistan were to go and have a look at the Afghan insurgency and the Pakistanis. My sense was that Chuck trusted me to come up with recommendations regarding the entire "Afghan issue." I appreciated the fact that he had given me a fairly long leash: since we had worked together very closely after he took over the Near East Division, particularly during the Iran rescue mission, my assumption was that he knew me well enough to trust my judgment.

I regarded that with both appreciation and the knowledge that it placed the burden on me of being responsible, thorough and careful. I was no flaming "let's go start a war" type; in fact quite the opposite. I had based my CIA reputation on being a careful, sensible and thorough operations officer. At the same time, I will admit to being aggressive in pursuit of realistic goals once they had been properly established.

In my view, my marching orders were to find answers to the following questions:

- Would the nascent Afghan insurgency against the Soviets be something that the insurgents were likely to maintain over a long haul? In other words, would the Afghans be willing to enter into a protracted battle with the Soviet invaders?
- Would the Pakistanis – meaning President Zia ul Haq – be supportive of a serious effort to support the Afghan insurgents with arms?
- If the answers to the above two questions were yes, what sort of lethal assistance, and in what quantities, did the Afghans require?

I planned to spend my first months in Islamabad attempting to answer these questions.

By way of background, there had long been in a liaison relationship with Pakistani military intelligence: the Inter-Services Intelligence Directorate – ISI for short. The chief of ISI in my day was Lt. General Akhtar Abdur Rahman, a Pathan himself, and the man to whom President Zia entrusted Pakistani dealings with CIA. Over the next years I would develop a close working relationship with General Akhtar, and would work closely with ISI.

My first responsibility was to get a sense of whether the Afghans were prepared to fight a long war against the Soviets. I knew that the varied tribes that inhabited Afghanistan were truculent and warlike crew: through history they had repelled many an invader. I also knew that

Afghans were so crooked, as the old saying went, that when they died you didn't bury them – you screwed them into the ground. These were not nice people: they were fundamentalist Muslims whose social codes favored a permanent state of semi-war with enemies real and imagined. For many Afghan tribals fighting was an end in itself, and their culture of individual bravery and heroism, always mingled with duplicity and subterfuge, strongly suggested that they would resist the Soviet invaders. On the other hand the British had long kept "their" Pathans in a relative state of quietude by buying them off. It was therefore entirely possible that the Soviets, who now occupied Afghanistan, if they adopted the British Indian policy of paying-off tribes to stay quiet, could successfully use the same techniques.

My ISI interlocutors told me that the Afghan tribals would fight the Soviets until hell froze over. In their mind this was the result of a combination of three things: their fundamentalist Islamic makeup, which held "godless communism" as abhorrent; their instinctive proclivity toward to warfare; and their refusal to give in to any invader, no matter who that might be. The latter two characteristics were fully documented in the history of British Indian dealings with the frontier tribals and Afghanistan in general.

Since I wanted to get my own feeling for the mood of Afghans (and the border tribes living between Pakistan and Afghanistan) towards the Soviet invaders, I made a number of trips to Peshawar, the city close to the Afghan border that was flooded with refugees from Afghanistan. My technique was simple: I simply wandered into the enormous Peshawar bazaar – which been in operation for well over 2,000 years – and talked to people. Since there were a number of Western journalists and aid workers in Peshawar, my being a foreigner did not prompt any particular surprise or suspicion. When I say talking to people I mean that literally, although it could be very difficult given the many language barriers involved. I remember many a conversation in which I would be attempting to talk to a tribesman from deep inside Afghanistan where I would have to go through two or three separate interpreters – there are that many languages in the geographic entity we refer to as Afghanistan. Some of these scenes were literally hilarious, with good humor on all sides.

My questions were simple and the first was: "why are you here?" The answer was inevitably "to get guns to fight the Russians."

Peshawar had long been the arms market for tribals inside and outside of Afghanistan. Mostly for homemade weapons produced in mud huts by the most extraordinarily talented gun makers in the world. Every Afghan had to carry a rifle: it was <u>the</u> obligatory badge of manhood. Rifles could be obtained in two ways – one could kill a "government soldier" (which was now very much out of fashion), or one could buy a homemade copy of the standard 20th century British firearm, the Lee Enfield .303 bolt action rifle. These were made largely from steel from melted down railway tracks. These "Khyber copies," (so nick-named because of Peshawar's proximity to the famous Khyber Pass,) more or less worked. Every tribal who possibly could afford to buy – or steal – a rifle would do so.

But, I was told, there were no guns except at the very high prices charged by local gun makers. Clearly there was a demand for weapons, and the more people with whom I talked, the larger that demand seemed to be.

So my next question was, obviously, "why do you want guns?" The answer, invariably, was "to kill Russians." These replies were utterly spontaneous, unrehearsed and heartfelt. Based on my small sample there were one hell of a lot of Afghans looking for weapons to go after the Soviets in Afghanistan.

My last question was usually something to the effect that since the Soviets had tanks, an Air Force, and many sophisticated weapons, how could men armed just with rifles take on such a massively better armed foe? The answer was usually a shrug, with a comment "Allah will provide."

These highly informal forays into the bazaar always came up with the same results. While hardly a massive national poll, after many an hour and many a meal with these Afghan refugees, I was persuaded that indeed, as ISI asserted, there was an enormous reservoir of Afghans determined to fight the Soviets. And, equally clearly, there were few weapons with which to fight.

I was convinced that "Afghans" were perhaps the most potentially dangerous guerrilla fighters in the world. They had that rare combination of social and religious mores that incline them to a long war – so long as that war could be fought on their terms. That meant that unlike a modern army, which would be deployed for an indefinite period, Afghans would drop in and out of warfare. They would fight for a few months, and then return to their safe havens in Pakistan. To me this seemed a perfectly sensible way to be a guerrilla, and they were going to have to fight a guerrilla war. It also seemed to me that if an individual and/or his group were prepared to go into Afghanistan for three or four months and then withdraw, the trick would be to have groups going in at about the same rate as groups were coming out. This, in fact, turned out to be how the war was fought. Weather also played a role: winter in some parts of Afghanistan brings almost intolerable cold, particularly in the mountainous areas, and this meant that the pace of fighting would drop significantly in winter. This too, it seemed to me, was a perfectly acceptable reality of the kind of warfare that the mujahedin would be fighting.

I, therefore, believed strongly that Afghans would indeed fight a protracted guerrilla war – but only if they had the arms with which to fight.

The next job was to assess how serious the Pakistanis were in terms of supporting the mujahedin. (Note: mujahedin was the universally-accepted term for the "freedom fighters," who I also call guerrillas and insurgents.)

I had long discussions with General Akhtar on the subject of <u>hypothetical</u> assistance to the mujahedin. There was no question in my mind: President Zia had instructed Akhtar to be very forward in responding to my questions by telling me that the Pakistanis were prepared to accept what I termed "significant supplies" of weapons, and to funnel those weapons to the mujahedin. In effect, Akhtar verbally committed to accepting some unspecified quantity of weaponry, and his organization would see that the weapons were delivered into the hands of the insurgents. I went over this a number of times with Akhtar, telling him that we did not want to start "the ball rolling" if the Pakistanis would subsequently renege. He was definitive in stating that it was Zia's long-term policy to provide weapons to the mujahedin. Akhtar also promised me verbally that ISI would be responsible for moving the weapons from wherever they arrived in Pakistan into Afghanistan. And that he was prepared to devote ISI personnel and other resources to any program that might subsequently develop.

Akhtar proved to be true to his word.

It is important to note that as of the summer of 1981, the only assistance that the Pakistanis had been able to provide to the insurgents was a small supply of .303 rifles. As Akhtar said, "we simply don't have the weapons to give away". It was clear from our surveys that weapons were indeed in desperately short supply, and that the Pakistanis were telling us the truth.

By the fall of 1981, I felt that I had answered the two primary questions: would the Afghan mujahedin fight, and would the Pakistanis serve as a conduit for the introduction of large supplies of weapons to them. Fortunately there was a senior-level conference attended by Chuck Cogan and John McGaffin in Bangkok that fall. I went to the conference with the express intention of telling Chuck of my findings, and suggesting that he set in motion requests for Presidential authorizations and funding to procure weapons for the insurgents. Both men were supportive of the entire concept, and cables began to flow back and forth. I, of course, depended utterly on Cogan and the McGaffin to do all the necessary bureaucratic work in Washington. Akhtar was jubilant, and even the sphinx-like Zia was visibly very pleased.

Soon thereafter, I received word that a program to arm the guerillas had been approved at the highest levels. We were in business, and I so informed Akhtar and President Zia.

In making my recommendations to Chuck Cogan, I had a very clear vision of what I saw as our objectives in Afghanistan. Since I believed that the Afghans would fight, and my studies and experience strongly suggested that they would continue to keep fighting into a distant and unknown future, I thought that the Soviets could be "punished" for their invasion of the country by a protracted series of losses, which cumulatively could have serious impact on what President Reagan called the "evil Empire."

The mujahedin could never, I reasoned, defeat the Soviets in the conventional sense of one army against another. Nor did they need to.

This would be a war of attrition, where the mujahedin, living in their millions in Pakistan, could bear their losses with far greater equanimity then could the Soviets. Over time, I reasoned, the Soviets would either have to accept such losses as a permanent feature of their occupation, or, as happened to us in Vietnam, finally decide that the pain was not worth bearing. The Soviets could and would remain in Afghanistan so long as their "pain level" was tolerable. Perhaps, I thought, a decade or two of fighting would eventually prove intolerable to the Soviet Union. That day was far off – if it ever came at all – but if one took the long view it was <u>not</u> an impossible outcome: again, witness our experience in Vietnam.

There was another consideration: the Afghan refugees in Pakistan wanted to fight to drive out the foreign invader. They deserved to be given the tools – weapons – that they needed for this fight. In a sense, I felt that the free world, and particularly the United States, was morally obliged to arm them.

I did not see the war as being "fought to the last Afghan": they were far too cunning and resilient a people to, as the phrase suggests, be obliterated by the Soviets. The Afghans themselves would determine the extent of their casualties, and there would always be enough insurgents to carry on the battle.

Finally, in considering this sort of protracted war, one had to remember that, by definition, every mujahedin who died was a "martyr" to the cause of Islam, and thus received an immediate ticket to Heaven. To the average Afghan there were far worse things than dying in the service of God.

Soon thereafter, I received word that a program to arm the guerrillas had been approved at the highest levels. We were in business, and I so informed Akhtar and President Zia. Akhtar was jubilant.

The next step was to draw up an initial list of weaponry to be procured and delivered to Pakistan for ISI to move to the insurgents. As I recall this "wish list," prepared in consultation with ISI, was a miracle of conservative thinking. Compared to what would soon be available it was a drop in the bucket. But it was an enormous increase over the pitiful amount of supplies the Pakistanis had made available to the mujahedin.

We sent the list back to Headquarters, it was approved, and the request funded. In a remarkably short time ships started turning up in Karachi harbor with loads of weapons and ammunition. I was quite proud of how CIA Headquarters went from a standstill to a dead run in procuring weapons for the operation. Akhtar was astonished at how quickly weapons began to arrive at Pakistan's major seaport, and he quickly had to make provision to offload the weaponry, place it on railcars, and move it to distribution points along the border with Afghanistan.

We decided early on that no American weapons would be used in the war. Aside from obsolete British rifles, our preference was for Soviet-designed weaponry, which the Agency obtained from a variety of sources – including from Eastern European countries, Egypt, and China. So long as I was involved with the war we would hold the line at using only foreign weapons. Initially, at least, this gave us some degree of "plausible denial," and in fact gave us a good deal more bang for the buck, as Soviet designed weapons could be had at knock-down prices.

The Afghan war had begun, and a short two years later Director Casey was able to make the extraordinary "battle damage" assessment of its effect on Soviet forces in Afghanistan that is noted at the start of this chapter.

In the three years of the insurgency when I was in charge, a tour that ended in the early summer of 1984, we went from no funding to a budget of over $250 million a year. In those years I depended utterly on Cogan and McGaffin to support our efforts, and I could not possibly have been in better hands. As a practical matter they left it to me to "run" the war on the ground, while they dealt with the many intricacies of Headquarters, Congress and Washington in general. There could have been no better arrangement. The Cogan/McGaffin duo left key decisions on almost all matters related to fighting the war in our hands: the theory being that we, in consultation with our Pakistani allies, were in the best position to know what would and would not work as we steadily increased pressure on the Soviet 40th Army in Afghanistan.

As the number of well-armed insurgents increased rapidly we knew that Soviet losses were mounting, a situation which from the Soviet perspective was unanticipated and something for which they had no answer.

It was still a secret war, and CIA was still in charge of it. Later, once its success became better known to an increasingly large number of people in Washington, more and more pressure would come from various quarters on CIA's program in Afghanistan. I was spared all of this.

One of my main tasks in Islamabad was to continue to develop and expand our working liaison relationship with the Pakistanis, which meant ISI.

The war turned into a massive logistics and an only slightly smaller training operation. The fact is that there was absolutely no way for us to support a major insurgency in Afghanistan without going through Pakistan. It was Pakistani territory through which weapons traveled into Afghanistan; and the Pakistani military assumed the entire burden of transporting the weapons and for training, where appropriate, guerrillas in their use. That became a huge effort on the Pakistani side, since weapons and ammunition are bulky. Literally train loads of weaponry had to be moved. Those train loads in turn had to be broken down into smaller "chunks" for transport by trucks, and those "chunks" broken down still further so that they would be transportable by pack animals or individual guerrillas.

As we moved from the provision of small arms – rifles – into supplying medium and heavy machine guns; rocket propelled grenades; recoilless rifles; mortars; mines; rockets and eventually antiaircraft missiles, the training workload on ISI grew exponentially. The ISI staff needed to handle all of these requirements grew rapidly, and more and more officers and soldiers were taken into the program.

My relations with Gen. Akhtar were excellent, and grew better over time. Akhtar was deeply distrusted in the Pakistan Army because he was known to be close to President Zia, and, after all, ISI also had the responsibility for keeping an eye out for any possible anti-Zia elements in the Pakistani Army. Akhtar was a vain and handsome man who many of his subordinate officers found overbearing and something of a martinet. He always treated me with courtesy and professional deference, and I in turn extended him every courtesy. At the same time we had a number of low key arguments about such things as which groups to support, and what sorts of weapons to procure, so there was a fair amount of healthy pushing and pulling in the relationship. We treated each other as partners, professionals involved in a very high-stakes power struggle. We were always very respectful of each other's "turf," and I knew that Akhtar reported to President Zia in great detail on the progress of the war, and on our relationship.

I found that one key to Akhtar was to make sure that all of our new ideas were his own. This often required a little fancy footwork, but it greatly eased the introduction of new concepts or activities. In general, however, we were much of the same mind over most things.

Akhtar's principal deputy was a Brigadier General named Raza, for whom I have nothing but the highest praise. Raza was a polite, soft-spoken, self-effacing officer with a brilliant mind and an impressive presence. He masterminded the logistics and training programs, and frequently dealt with the mujahedin groups in Peshawar. Personally attractive and absolutely honest, the Brigadier was an enormous asset to the entire endeavor. His participation in the program was very reassuring, since we did not believe that such an officer could or would act to deceive us in any way.

It would be very difficult to overstate Brigadier Raza's contribution. While Akhtar selfishly took the credit, it was Raza who actually made things happen. I assumed that is why President Zia placed Raza in ISI: Zia knew Akhtar to be in many ways incompetent and unimaginative, and Raza was to be the man behind the scenes doing the actual work. The ultimate defeat of the Soviet Union's invasion of Afghanistan owes a great deal to General Raza's extraordinary competence and utter dedication.

Liaison relationships such as this can be very tricky, particularly when the Pakistanis were justifiably anxious that we not somehow abuse our rather unusual position. For my part, I was very aware that while we were utterly dependent on the Pakistanis to make the insurgency possible, it was important that we be treated as equal partners. I always had the feeling that this was the case. Pakistani sensitivities were an important concern, certainly so long as General Akhtar and President Zia were alive. (Both of these men were killed when a Pakistan Air

Force C-130 aircraft mysteriously blew up some years after I departed Pakistan. My assumption has always been that this was done at the direction of the Soviet KGB in Kabul and/or Islamabad. To add to the tragedy, the American Ambassador and most of the senior commanders of the Pakistani military, all of whom were on the same aircraft, were also killed.)

I had strong views on how a guerrilla war should (and should not) be fought. In some significant measure these views came from my youth, when I listened to Americans who had been guerrilla leaders in the Philippines in World War II – I profited from their experiences. I remembered war stories from Chick Parsons and his peers: practical advice in the "do's and don'ts" of guerrilla warfare. In addition, I had read a great many books on the subject, including many written by former British Indian Army officers who had served on the Frontier with Afghanistan. I also studied analyses of our experience in Vietnam before the North Vietnamese Army entered the war.

Conventional military men have a real problem understanding how guerrillas can and should operate. For example, I had one visitor from the Department of Defense who told me categorically that the mujahedin should be capturing and holding territory inside Afghanistan. Such assertions are and were absurd, since by definition doing that would enable the Soviets to bring to bear their much greater strength, particularly in airpower, armor and artillery, all of which the mujahedin lacked. I reminded him of the disastrous French experience at Dien Bien Phu during France's war in Indochina. He seemed to have real trouble understanding that what Soviet commanders in Afghanistan would most like to see was a large gathering of mujahedin determined to defend a given piece of territory.

What we and the Pakistanis agreed on were tactics that involved the insurgents making hit-and-run attacks: for example, striking at Soviet vehicles moving on the very limited roadways in Afghanistan – and then disappearing into the wilderness. Whatever else, the mujahedin were to avoid pitched fixed battles with the Soviets.

One of the techniques that I used in considering both the strategy and tactics of this guerrilla war was to try to place myself in the mind of the commander of the Soviet 40th Army, which was the occupying force in Afghanistan. It seemed to me that by doing this I could sense his vulnerabilities and his strengths, and thus better fashion our own activities. I knew that he was a conventional military commander whose training, doctrine and strategy was geared to a full scale war – not a conflict with guerrillas. He had enormous assets at his disposal, just as we had had in the guerrilla war days in South Vietnam. But, given the size of Afghanistan and the amount of territory that he had to "secure," I knew that he had only limited choices for how to use those assets. The Soviets had deployed around 110,000 troops to Afghanistan, a number that remained constant through my entire period of involvement with the war. He did not have sufficient forces to cover the entire country, and he certainly did not have enough force to seal off the routes that the insurgents used to move themselves and their weapons from Pakistan into Afghanistan. That long and ill-defined border was literally absolutely porous to insurgent movements. The mujahedin could, by and large, enter and exit Afghanistan at will.

It was always my assumption that the Soviet commander had asked for and had been denied a force adequate to both police the border and to defend the cities and the main transportation routes in the country. My guess was that he would need at least 400,000 troops to do an effective job of shutting down insurgent supply routes into the country, while he at the same time was defending major population centers and his own bases. So long as he did not receive this huge additional force I felt we had him between a rock and a hard place. As Soviet casualties mounted I suspect that he screamed more and more often for really significant increases in Soviet troops – requests that were denied by Moscow. I did not envy his position, and I was determined that we could use his limitations to our advantage; which was, in fact, exactly what the insurgents did.

I also had to consider the size and composition of our "own forces," the mujahedin. My rough guess was that as of early 1984, we had armed around 400,000 insurgents – Afghans who had weapons and were committed to fighting inside the country. This very large number of fighters was, of course, subject to their mode of operations, which was to drop in and out of the fighting. My very subjective guess was that at any one time we probably had around 40,000 guerrillas in country busily attacking Soviet forces. This number would increase in the summer when the weather was better. Assuming that I was in the ballpark when it came to the number of Afghans actively "at war," and the realities of the way the Afghans sensibly chose to fight their war – rotating into and out of the country – I was quite content.

One of the major issues that arose in my day and persisted through the course of the war was the question of the "boiling pot." This was President Zia's chosen metaphor: keep the pot boiling but never let it boil over. "Boiling over" in the metaphor meant prompting an adverse Soviet response against Pakistan, possibly including military attacks on the country. Each time we introduced a new type of weapon this issue came up, as it did when we discussed the amount of weaponry that should be passed to the insurgents.

A good case in point was the introduction of heavy machine guns. We noted that the Soviets made extensive use of helicopter gunships, which, to maximize their effectiveness, flew at very low altitudes over known or suspected mujahedin positions. We decided that if we equipped the insurgents with heavy machine guns we could bring down enough of their helicopters to force them to fly at much higher altitudes – and thus greatly reduce their effectiveness. Assuming we were right in concluding that we could cause significant casualties to the Soviet helicopter gunship fleet, this would represent a significant increase in the rate at which "the pot boiled." Akhtar was initially reluctant to take this step but after we hammered at it long enough he agreed, and with Zia's concurrence a large number of heavy machine guns were procured and inserted into Afghanistan. Sure enough, we quickly noted a significant increase in gunship "kills," and saw the Soviet helicopters flying at much higher altitudes.

Possession of these heavy weapons also enabled the insurgents to "bait" Soviet gunships into positions where concealed machine guns could take them out. And the same weapons were used with great effect against unarmored or lightly armored Soviet vehicles.

We repeated this incremental increase in the types and quantity of weapons several times. For example, we subsequently introduced a not very efficient shoulder-fired, man-portable, Chinese made anti-aircraft missile. The point here was to drive both the helicopter gunships and fixed wing fighter-bomber aircraft of the Soviet Air Force even higher – with a corresponding reduction in their effectiveness. It did not matter very much whether the missiles were terribly effective – they were not – but no pilot wants to see a missile flying up at him. This also had the intended results.

This was another increase in the temperature of the pot, without its boiling over.

We also introduced recoilless rifles: in effect portable artillery pieces, which the insurgents could use with great effect against Soviet armor. And we inserted a variety of Soviet-designed ground-to-ground rockets which provided an excellent "stand- off" weapon for use against Soviet airfields, destroying a large number of Soviet aircraft on the ground in the process.

This mix of weapons made the mujahedin a vastly more powerful and effective force, with corresponding increases in insurgent morale, while the Soviets suffered steadily increasing losses.

Director Casey visited Islamabad three times during my watch, when he met with President Zia and Gen. Akhtar. Casey was greatly taken by the insurgency, as this was "stuff" he really understood: killing the Soviet invaders. One of the inevitable results of a Casey visit was his request to visit an actual mujahedin training camp and the Khyber Pass. I was not about to be the first CIA officer to lose a Director of Central Intelligence, and on his first visit I was able to deflect this by telling him that the training camps were too close to the Afghan border and the Khyber Pass area was alive with armed communist Afghans, which was the truth. On his second visit he got a good deal huffier about his desire to visit the training camps. This time I enlisted the aid of Gen. Akhtar, who was honestly appalled at the idea of Casey going anywhere near the Afghan border, and absolutely forbade such travel.

On Casey's third visit I knew what was coming, and Akhtar and I worked out a slightly deceptive scheme. We briefly relocated a complete Afghan training camp to an area close to Islamabad, and took Casey to it – after driving aimlessly in circles for more than two hours to indicate that we were some distance from the city. In the dead of night, in a dimly lit training camp, Casey got to see – and touch – real live mujahedin being trained in the use of the heavy weapons that we were inserting into Afghanistan. The scene literally brought tears to the old man's eyes.

The Afghan war was not, of course, the only activity that we were involved in. Pakistan was making rapid strides towards developing nuclear weapons, and it was our job to keep a finger on their weapons program – which we did. Essentially President Reagan and Congress chose to turn a blind eye to the Pakistani nuclear program in exchange for their cooperation with us in fighting the Soviets.

Our reporting on nuclear matters was very sensitive and closely controlled; however, the subject fairly often came up in the *New York Times*, which seemed to have excellent sources in Washington. Every time some new press article that reported on Pakistani nuclear weapons development came up, I was called down by Gen. Akhtar, who protested that such stories were false. Akhtar would accuse me of feeding false information to Washington on nuclear matters: I would deny having had anything to do with such stories. This developed into something of a pro forma series of protests and denials by both sides. In a way it was kind of amusing since both the Pakistanis and I knew what the truth was. The subject could have had a really adverse effect on our working relationship with the Pakistanis and on the war in Afghanistan, and it was my job to see that it did not. I am convinced that had the administration and/or Congress sought to make a real issue of the nuclear matter by taking punitive action against Pakistan, we would have lost the ability to keep the war against the Soviets going.

This was always an interesting and delicate matter: it was our job to report on nuclear matters while at the same time keeping our relationship with the Pakistanis on an even keel so that we could continue to fight and expand the war in Afghanistan.

Another focus of the Agency's collection program was related to Soviet weapons. Since Afghanistan was the first occasion when regular military forces were deployed outside of the Soviet Union, Soviet troops came equipped with equipment that we had not seen before, and that the Soviets had never sold to their foreign clients. What we were seeing was the equipment in use by first-line Soviet infantry and air forces, and there was a huge requirement for us to obtain samples of this equipment.

Some of our findings were real shocks to the weapons people in Washington. It turned out, for example, that Soviet antitank rockets were far more efficient then what we had previously seen, with potentially immediate and unhappy consequences to U.S. armed forces. Another example was the armored vests – "flak jackets" – worn by Soviet troops, particularly the *Spetsnatz* (Special Forces) units: we were told that these jackets, once we had obtained examples of them, were far superior to our own. We would collect fairly large quantities of this Soviet "ordnance," both with help from the Pakistanis and on our own, and we always took some pride in showing Director Casey what we had collected.

Our accumulation of Soviet weaponry, particularly the high explosive versions, gave me a permanent nightmare. There was always a concern that they would blow up, which would definitely not be a good thing. While we stashed these goodies in the safest the places we could, and did not fiddle around with them, I was always hugely relieved when Headquarters would send us armorers who would render the weapons "safe" before shipping them back to the States. On one occasion we obtained a complete Soviet combat vehicle, which our military was so anxious to get their hands on that they had a C-141 transport fly into Islamabad to pick it up.

Obtaining this Soviet ordnance, some of which was more than a little frightening, was a real coup, and I am sure that we gave whoever it was in the United States who tested and analyzed these weapons a ton of work to do.

Casey's last visit came near the end of my tour in the summer of 1984. At the airport on his departure Casey said that he would prefer that I remained in Pakistan for another year. I begged him not to order the Director of Operations to extend my tour past the usual three years. My reasoning was simple: first and foremost I did not want him to overrule one of the Service's personnel mandates. Second, both John McGaffin and Chuck Cogan were leaving their respective jobs at Headquarters, and I knew that there would be a very significant change in the tone and tenor of my relationship with my colleagues in Washington. Third, it had been a very hard three years, and I was growing weary of playing "field marshal." Finally, I thought that it was time that a different set of hands took the wheel – it would be a good opportunity to take a new and different look at the program.

I also had the sense that a sea change was taking place in Washington: too many outside players were trying to horn in on the operation that we had been running so successfully for three years. I was getting signals that some massive new emphasis was going to be placed on expanding the program, an emphasis which I thought might not bode well for its success. Indeed, that is exactly what happened: a great many more cooks with endless amounts of money arrived in the kitchen, with not altogether positive results.

I left Islamabad in the summer of 1984 with rather mixed feelings. On the one hand I felt that I had earned my keep over the preceding three years, and I took a certain amount of pride in the fact that we had started and were now running a very effective war against the Soviet Union. I felt that it was very important that we were punishing the Soviets for having invaded a foreign country which very clearly wanted no part of them. Perhaps, thought I, this would dissuade them from some other adventure in another country. It was also pay-back in some degree for the Soviet support of North Vietnam – support which had cost us so dearly in the Vietnam War. A little retribution was a good thing.

On the other hand it was hard to leave: it had been a real journey.

After my departure the war grew in size as ever more money and ever more complicated weapons were introduced into Afghanistan. The war continued for five more years, at the end of which the Soviets departed. I have always been hugely amused – and occasionally a little annoyed – by how many people have claimed that they ran and won the war in Afghanistan: particularly by those in CIA who came years later and inherited a full-blown and growing war. The old truth that "victory has many fathers" certainly came into play.

The truth is that the Afghan freedom fighters won the war. And not just the war in Afghanistan – witness the following statement by Eduard Shevardnadze, the last Minister of Foreign Affairs of the Soviet Union (1985-91.)

"The Afghan war was the last nail in the coffin of the Soviet Union."

10

THE COUNTER NARCOTICS CENTER

Before leaving Islamabad I had an onward assignment but, to my surprise, I received a message from Director Casey a few days before departing Pakistan: the assignment that I expected to be going to was "broken," and Casey politely instructed me to take – in yet another directed assignment – a job that was the last thing in the world that I expected. It was a job in a "sensitive" area of the NCS, and one that I am constrained not to discuss. Once again the "needs of the service" prevailed. I was occupied with this position for what I expected to be a two-year term. However, after 18 months on the job I was once again called to Casey's office and given another job – this time running the NCS's paramilitary operations division. I was beginning to feel a bit like a tennis ball being batted back and forth across the net.

The difficult part of these assignments was that they took the incumbents who I replaced by surprise, and I was dropped in as though from outer space to replace them. Casey clearly regarded me as something of a "fixer" of units of the NCS that he did not think were up to snuff. I realized that each such surprise assignment would no doubt earn me a certain amount of enmity, but I was as surprised as anyone else, so I just went about whatever my new business was.

I was at these two jobs until 1987, when I received word that I had been appointed Chief of Station in a major European country, perhaps our largest station. My wife, Jean, and I proceeded overseas in 1988. Unfortunately, after only a few months on the job I became ill, and had to return to Washington. As the doctors were not sure how long recovery would take, my assignment was canceled.

After a couple of months I was back on my feet again, and I was called in to meet with the Director, now Judge William Webster. Judge Webster had previously been director of the FBI, and had come to CIA at the instruction of President George H. W. Bush. I had met him in the course of my previous assignments, and had come to have a great deal of respect for him. The quiet soft-spoken Judge was about as different from Bill Casey as it was possible to be, and I came to admire him for the way he carried out his responsibilities as Director of Central Intelligence (DCI.)

Judge Webster told me that the President, who had once been DCI himself, had directed Webster to figure out some way that the Foreign Intelligence Community, with all of its resources, could assist in the war on drugs, which the President had very correctly defined as a national security threat.

In those days the DCI had two jobs – first to run the CIA, and second to be the senior officer "presiding" over the other intelligence agencies in the Community.

President Bush had appointed a "drug czar," Bill Bennett, to lead and coordinate all federal activities in support of the "war on drugs." That war was not going well, and President Bush believed – correctly – that the enormous resources of the various foreign intelligence agencies could in some manner be used to assist our law enforcement agencies; but only as it concerned drug matters <u>overseas.</u>

Judge Webster asked me, while I was still more or less convalescing, to put my mind to devising a plan on just how this might be done.

Given this new charge, I begged an office in which to work, and set about drawing up a proposal to accomplish what President Bush wanted. I spent a few weeks devising a plan for Judge Webster's consideration, and had completed the task at about the same time that the medics cleared me for full-time duty.

It is important to note that the agencies involved in the Foreign Intelligence (FI) Community are barred by law from operating in the United States. Therefore the question was how the many capabilities of FI agencies could be of maximum assistance to the law enforcement agencies which, working both domestically and overseas, carried the main burden of combating the international drug menace.

I had assumed that the task Judge Webster had given me was an interim one, and that once I had submitted my proposals to him I would no longer be involved with the project – if indeed the Judge agreed with the structure that I had created on paper. I recall that when I gave him the plan I commented that whoever might be responsible for executing it was, because of the inter-Agency nature of the proposal, going to have an absolutely thankless task.

Webster reviewed my submission, called me back in, told me that he had accepted the plan in its entirety – and that I was to implement it as rapidly as possible.

What I had come up with was the concept of creating a "Counter Narcotics Center" (CNC) that would amalgamate appropriate parts of the various agencies in the FI Community <u>with</u> the Federal law enforcement agencies busy fighting the "drug war." In addition to people skilled in analysis and NCS "operators" in the field, the Center would contain people from the Agency's scientific and technical Directorate in order to bring their expertise to bear on the drug problem.

So that this not be viewed as a CIA power grab, I defined the Center as reporting to the DCI wearing his FI Community "hat." It would be physically located in CIA, as that was the fastest way to obtain "quarters and rations" since the DCI controlled CIA's resources.

In brief, I envisaged CNC as combining in one place a large group of analysts - all from CIA, which already had a fair number of people working on narcotics issues; with CIA operations types from the NCS, many of whose stations were working in some manner on the drug problem. They would be joined by personnel from the Agency's Scientific and Technical Directorate in order to bring to bear their advanced technical collection capabilities. We would then add representatives from each of the several Federal law enforcement services into the mix. CNC would become a "one stop" central point in which everyone in the drug war would be represented, working together to maximize the impact of all our resources.

CNC would also represent the Foreign Intelligence Community at the National Security Council's (NSC) working group on counter narcotics, and work closely with the office of the "drug czar." I came to value this NSC role, as its chairman, Ambassador David Miller, brought a high level of enthusiasm and professionalism, and having strong NSC support for all of our efforts was a real shot in the arm. Ambassador Miller was responsible for setting up several trips in White House aircraft to the key "drug countries" in the Andean region. These were important opportunities for us to meet with Embassy and DEA personnel, and for us to get a better feel for the local situation: "ground truth." David's ebullient good humor and optimism frequently got us through depressing times in a "war" in which we seemed unable to have many victories. David was a real cheerleader for CNC, as he had a clear understanding of what our mission was and the resource CNC represented. We became good friends, which we remain today.

I will never forget an incident on one of our trips. We flew to a remote jungle outpost where the local army, under the direction of DEA, was searching out narco's and their cocaine labs. In honor of our visit the local army commander had drawn up all his troops for inspection, and David, as our senior officer, got to do the inspecting. There was something surreal about standing around in a jungle clearing while David passed up and down the lines of assembled troops, looking very serious with his best military face on. The rest of us had to struggle not to grin.

The way I had designed the Center seemed to me to be a fairly straightforward approach to improving our response to the many threats posed by the international narcotics cartels. Interestingly enough, CNC later became the model for a number of "Centers" working on various key problems. For example, there soon came into existence a Counterterrorism Center and a Center concerned with the spread of weapons of mass destruction.

The first task was to physically establish the Center, drawing in people scattered about in various offices and buildings all over the CIA complex. In this task, which was quite outside any experience that I'd ever had in the Agency, I was blessed to have a Deputy who was a master at harnessing the bureaucracy. Dave Carey came to me from the Directorate of Intelligence – under whose wing I had placed the Center. Dave had a brilliant mind and encyclopedic knowledge of how the

Headquarters bureaucracy works. In addition, he was one of the nicest men I'd ever met. His contribution to the establishment and functioning of the Center cannot possibly be overstated. He would return several years later to run the Center himself, and eventually would be promoted to the job of the Agency's Executive Director; the number three man in CIA, whose brief was to run the Agency day-to-day. Without David we simply could not have gotten CNC up and running as quickly and efficiently as we did. I owe him an everlasting debt of gratitude, and to this day count him as one of my closest friends.

It turned out that the only possible space to place the entire Center together in the main Headquarters building was in the basement, which of course was windowless. Small price to pay, I thought, in order to have all of us in one place. There was actually no choice in this matter, and in the end the office spaces provided to us were quite satisfactory. Having all of the sections of the Center together resulted in a much more effective and collegial work atmosphere.

There was, of course, some joking (and relatively little bitching) about our physical location, and I remember when some wag asked if this was not the ultimate extension of the Agency's "mushroom theory of management: "keep them in the dark, cover them with shit, and cut their heads off once a year." I earnestly assured them that this was exactly right.

While Dave Carey was busily assembling a Center that would eventually turn out to involve hundreds of people, it was my job to go to the other agencies in Washington that we wanted to provide representation to the Center. I knew this was going to be a real trick, as no Agency wants to send people to another Agency, and there was always the suspicion that CNC was the proverbial camel sticking its nose under the tent. I had a rapid education in inter-Agency suspicions, as "turf protection" was the guiding principle everywhere I went. And some agencies couldn't stand each other, never mind CIA. For example, there was a running battle between DEA and the FBI, where the FBI took the position that DEA was a subordinate organization that was running out from underneath its hat: an enmity that was wholeheartedly returned by DEA. My job was to persuade the heads of all the concerned agencies that it was in their best interest to send a handful of representatives to the Center, and that they could and should expect to receive a high rate of return on their investment.

I took the high road when it came to dealing with the heads of the various agencies we wanted to participate in the Center. This included, first and foremost, the Drug Enforcement Administration (DEA), followed by the FBI, Customs, NSA, and several other key agencies that were involved in some way in the drug war. By taking the high road I mean that I simply went to the heads of the various agencies and very politely said that I was operating under a mandate from both the DCI and the President, and that I assumed that each Agency head understood that we were all bound to observe that mandate. While there were some initial reservations, we were quickly able to obtain the representation we needed, and in a matter of a few months the Center was up and running.

When I began this assignment I knew nothing about the "drug problem" as it impacted the United States, and I was in for a very steep learning curve. I soon came to believe that the threat posed to the country by imported narcotics was a deeply serious one. We were up against a tremendously well-organized and brutal enemy – the international drug cartels. I also was quickly persuaded that we were desperately short of intelligence on these cartels; and that we needed to make a serious contribution to attacking the cartels by supporting both unilateral (i.e., by DEA and CIA) operations, and through liaison with various intelligence services and military organizations around the world, particularly in Latin America.

One of CNC's first responsibilities was to try to get a handle on the size of the drug threat to the United States. This was an issue that could directly be addressed by CNC with its foreign intelligence capabilities. It was the first of many such issues where our resources were vastly greater than that of the law enforcement agencies, and where we could provide really outstanding assistance.

DEA had estimated that something like 50 metric tons of cocaine entered the United States each year. This estimate was a very rough one, and largely depended upon the number of seizures of cocaine that DEA made in the United States. My analysts were of the view that this seriously understated the quantity of drugs that were available to enter the country. One of the Center's first tasks therefore was to survey all of Latin America to see how much coca – the plant from which cocaine is made – was being grown. To accomplish this we ordered reconnaissance aircraft to photograph the continent's coca growing areas. The results of the study of this photography by the Center's analysts were staggering: given certain assumptions about how much cocaine could be produced from a given area under cultivation, the analysts concluded that something on the order of 800 metric tons of cocaine could be produced. When we passed this information to the White House, DEA and the "drug Czar," they were astonished.

Since one could assume that coca Farmers were selling their products, and that the cartels were refining raw coca into cocaine, the magnitude of cocaine available to the world market was absolutely staggering. The problem was far worse than any of us had anticipated.

It was clear that CIA and DEA offices in Latin America had to increase their efforts, and I made several trips to Latin America to convey our new findings, and to urge both agencies to devote more time and resources to the problem. This raised the issue of cooperation overseas between CIA and DEA, and I took on the job of identifying where there were problems and made efforts to improve the situation.

We also met with foreign liaison services to apprise them of our findings. Since so much cocaine was entering the world market it was clearly not all going to the United States, and I made several trips to Europe to talk with our liaison partners there to acquaint them with the magnitude of the threat. At the time our assertions were met with considerable skepticism, as several of the senior intelligence people I talked to did not believe that cocaine was a problem in their country. As politely as I could I tried to remedy this misconception. Time was to prove us right, and having rubbed their noses in it had some benefit in that the Europeans began to acknowledge the existence of the threat.

As we learned more about the drug cartels and their methods of operation, it was easy to see why they were working with relative impunity, particularly in Latin America. To say that these are brutal organizations is an understatement. It became clear, for example, how the cartels were able to suborn foreign officials and thus radically reduce the threat posed to them by Latin American counter narcotics organizations, both military and police.

It was, for example, common practice for a cartel representative to approach a Colombian police officer with an offer of a large amount of cash in return for the officers' cooperation. If that was not a hard enough temptation to resist, the cartel would at the same time tell the police officer that if he did not cooperate the cartel would kill his family; which they would do unless the officer cooperated. In other words, the cartels were operating with the utmost reliance on violence, real and threatened. In some countries the cartels had so penetrated the police and intelligence organizations ostensibly directed against them as to render those organizations utterly ineffective.

Our operations people, fully supported by analysts and our technical guys, began a series of efforts to target specific individuals in specific drug cartels. Sometimes this can be done unilaterally, but very often, perhaps usually, it involved the closest possible cooperation with intelligence, police, and military liaison services. It was always tricky to do this, since we had to assume that the foreign services with whom we were working were deeply penetrated by the "narcos." This meant some very careful work with the leaders of these foreign organizations in helping them to circumvent such penetrations.

One thing the Center did was provide "target intelligence" to the counter narcotics units of various South American countries. For example, in Columbia the cartels maintained their cocaine laboratories in the triple-canopy jungles, almost invisible to aerial reconnaissance. Our analysts learned to look for tip-offs that enabled them to zero in on these cocaine labs – information which we passed to DEA and/or to our liaison contacts to enable them to strike at the labs. I have a photograph of such a strike: where a local counter narcotics unit was burning a huge mound of cocaine, worth, according to DEA, roughly US$60 million at street prices in the United States.

While talking about prices, the flow of cocaine into the United States was so great that DEA informed us that the price of one "dose" of crack cocaine in the country was about the same price as a McDonald's hamburger. We learned another interesting fact: if you had five used

$20 bills three of them would have traces of cocaine on them – such was the frequency of cocaine use.

It's worth noting that CNC was not out to discover fire and invent the wheel; much was already being done against the drug threat, so our job was to get maximum return for all the effort that was being expended in the drug war. In terms of liaison, the business of building trustworthy liaison capabilities was a long-term effort which would take several years to bring to fruition. Neither Rome nor an effective counter narcotics effort could be built in a day.

There were occasional moments of humor in what was otherwise a busy and complicated work environment. As word of CNC's existence got around Washington, and as it appeared that we had funds to finance counter-narcotics activities, we received a steady succession of supplicants for money. A group from the Department of Agriculture turned up with what on the surface seem like a great idea. They had bred a species of moth which ate only coca plants. Their idea was to release these single-minded moths in coca growing areas, where they would promptly eat up the entire crop, and then presumably expire from want of food.

My question was whether the breeders of this moth could guarantee that, in fact, the insects would not morph into 200 pound carnivores, which would eat everything and everyone in the area where they were released. They of course could not. I decided we wanted no part of the insect wars.

Being Washington, someone quickly leaked the fact that I had turned down what on the surface appeared to be a great idea, and a marvelous cartoon appeared in one of the newspapers showing a CIA airplane flying over a Farmer, dropping moths. This prompted a call from the DCI who asked me if there was some truth to what was portrayed in the cartoon. I assured him that there was not, and said that the main problem was that we couldn't devise parachutes that were small enough to drop the moths. As soon as I hung up the phone I knew I'd made a mistake – and sure enough, I got an immediate call from his secretary to report to his office. I had to eat a little humble crow over my bad joke.

One of the things that most impressed me while I ran the Center was the dedication and competence of our analysts. I had had little opportunity in my years in the NCS to have close contacts with analysts. I discovered them to be highly imaginative when it came to using data available to them, and incredibly competent in seeing small indicators of very large problems. For example, in Peru a group of terrorists were supporting themselves by participating in the cocaine trade. Our analysts actually identified jungle training camps used by these terrorists: information which we passed on to the Peruvian government to help it attack the camps.

CNC analysts had previously been scattered about on their own in various buildings, far removed from "consumers" of the intelligence they produced. Having our analysts literally rubbing shoulders with both our operations and high-tech people paid frequent dividends. The analysts became more "operational," and our NCS and technical people became more "analytical" – to everyone's advantage.

Our technical section also made significant contributions. Their instructions were to think out of the ballpark, which they did, and they came up with a number of highly imaginative high tech schemes to both identify the locations where cocaine was stored and to track its movement into the US.

By the time I left CNC – after two years on the job - to go into retirement, I very strongly believed that thanks to the hard work of all the people involved – both Agency and people on detail to us from other agencies – we were making a significant contribution to the drug war. It was because of the fine performance of everyone involved in CNC that we both proved the basic concept of a "center" and were recognized as a major player in the war against narcotics. I was very proud to have had some part in building the Center and in its operation, and I tried hard to thank everyone involved in it.

11

POSTSCRIPT

I had decided in my late 30's that I would retire from the Agency when I was 50, which NCS personnel can do if they have a certain number of years of overseas service. I felt that I'd had a truly rewarding career, and there were no other jobs in the Agency that I wanted to take on. I announced my retirement a couple of months after my 50th birthday – much to the surprise of certain of my colleagues, who thought that I had been scrambling to climb the promotion ladder, and were astonished at my departure. In early 1991 I left "the building" feeling that I had done my bit, and that it was now time to do other things.

I had given one life to my country, and it was now time for a life of my own.

After retiring and moving to our home on top of the Blue Ridge in Virginia, my wife and I opened a consulting business that proved to be very successful, and we built a new and happy life. Unfortunately, the results of the beating I received in Tehran surfaced many years later, and required a series of operations to rearrange several of my internal organs, which had been damaged. This forced me to shut down our consultancy, and has greatly restricted by mobility.

We spent many years building a significant U.S. Martial Arms Collection, which we have donated to the Virginia War Memorial in Richmond, Virginia, and the National World War II Museum in New Orleans, Louisiana. We have viewed these weapons as our "connection" to Americans who have fought our wars from the War of Independence to our modern wars, and our role as stewards.

Iran and Afghanistan continue to be in the news. I am disheartened by the decision on the part of two presidents to attempt to fight a "nation building" war in Afghanistan. The Afghan mujahedin continued to fight us for the same reasons they fought the Soviets, and with equal success. Iran is on the verge of obtaining nuclear weapons, with potentially adverse consequences to peace in that part of the world.

In looking back at the CIA career, I wouldn't change a thing: it was a privilege to serve. My abiding hope is that the Agency will be able to continue to play the same successful role in defending American freedom as it has in the past.

I close with my favorite CIA toast: *To present company and absent friends.*

The End